Honey from the Comb

Honey from the Comb

A Guide to Focused Prayer Using Scripture

Compiled with Notes by
LeAnne Hardy

Birch Island Books
St. Paul, MN

Copyright © 2020 LeAnne Hardy
All rights reserved.
ISBN-13: 9798671909869

No part of this book may be reproduced, stored in a retrieval system, or transmitted in any form or by any means—electronic, mechanical, digital, photographic, recording, or any other—except for brief quotations in reviews, without the prior permission of the author.

Scriptures taken from the Holy Bible, New International Version ®, NIV®. Copyright© 1973, 1978, 1984, 2011 by Biblica, Inc.™. Used by permission of Zondervan. All rights reserved worldwide.
Grant No: Z34009

www.zondervan.com

Acknowledgements

Honey from the Comb began in the 1990s when I was challenged to pray through the attributes of God in my personal worship. My original list came from Arthur W. Pink's classic *The Attributes of God*. Over the years I added to it, and collected verses to focus my prayers. Since this collection of verses was originally intended only for personal use, I was not careful to keep track of sources. My apologies to preachers and writers whose ideas may have crept unacknowledged into these pages.

I would be remiss if I did not acknowledge my debt to my parents. My father, Dr. Charles F. Smith, has a heart for discipleship. He regularly took us aside after supper to study the Bible and discuss how it applied to our lives in specific ways. My mother, Letha Stuart Smith, modeled total commitment to the Lord in every aspect of life. She even told me once that she never entered a shopping mall without asking God to help her to choose wisely and exercise good stewardship of what he had given her.

My thanks also to my husband, Steve, who encouraged my times alone with the Lord by bringing me tea in bed.

LH

Table of Contents

Acknowledgements 5
Table of Contents 7
Preface 11
Introduction 13

Part I Adoration 17

The Almighty 21
The Comforter 23
The Covenant Maker 26
The Creator 28
Eternal God 31
Our Father 33
Faithful Promise Keeper 35
The Firstborn 37
Generous Provider 39
The Glorious One 42
Goodness Itself 44
Gracious God 46
Our Great High Priest 48
The Holy One of Israel 50
Hope of the Nations 52
Humble Servant 55
Immanuel, God with Us 57
Just Judge 59
King of Kings 62
The All-Knowing 64
Lamb of God 66
Source of Life 68
Love 71
Merciful Judge 73
The Only God 75
Patient Lord 77
The Ever-Present One 79
Our Refuge 81

God of Revelation 83
The Lord, Our Righteousness 85
Our Savior 87
The Good Shepherd 89
The Sovereign Lord 91
Spirit 93
The Suffering Servant 96
God of All Truth 98
The Unchanging One 100
The Way 102
Wise God 104
The Word made Flesh 106
God of Wrath 108

Part II: Confession 111

Ten Commandments 117
A Higher Law 119
Beatitudes 121
Such Were Some of You 123
My Thoughts and Attitudes 125
More about My Thought Life 128
Acts of the Sinful Nature 130
How I Treat Others 132
Love in Action 134
Renewing Relationships 137
Avoiding the Suggestion of Evil 139
Prayer of National Confession 141
Prayer of David 144

Part III: Thanksgiving 147

For Your Salvation 151
For Spiritual Blessings 152
For His Care 153
For Fellow Believers 154
For What God is Doing in the World 156
For Answered Prayer 157
For Wealth and Honor 159
For Restored Health 161

For God's Great Wonders 163
For Deliverance from sin 165
For Deliverance from Death 166
For God's Reign 168

Part IV: Supplication 169

Compassion 173
Contentment 175
Contrition 177
Courage 180
Diligence 183
Faith 186
Faithfulness 189
Forgiveness 191
Generosity 193
Goodness 196
Gratitude 198
Holiness 200
Humility 202
Integrity 205
Joy 207
Kindness 209
Love 211
Obedience 213
Patience 215
Peace 217
Perseverance 219
Purity 221
Righteousness 223
Self-control 225
Self-denial 227
Submission 230
Trust 233
Wisdom 235

Preface

Without doubt, I consider prayer the greatest privilege and the greatest weakness in my life. I have long been troubled with the imbalance and shallowness of my own prayers, and that of the church, which easily narrows to prayers of supplication, and that often selfishly or for things of lesser importance. That's not to say anything is too small to take to the Lord in prayer, but that we need to learn to pray for that which is of greatest concern to God.

To combat that imbalance, I've tried to pray as I read Scripture with the balance of biblical themes. I often encourage small prayer groups to start without asking God for anything; rather to focus on God, not ourselves, with Adoration and Thanksgiving; then to include Confession of sin individually and corporately before making any requests of God. If only I could be more consistent in following my own counsel.

In an effort to combat shallowness, I've found a few prayer tools to be of significant help such as *The Valley of Vision* by Arthur G. Bennett, and more recently, *Piercing Heaven* by Robert Elmer; both works collections of written prayers of the old Puritans. Yet even these great helps do not compare to the discipline and power of Scripture as the primary prayer tool. Yet we need models to help us. How do we transform and strengthen our prayers to be God-saturated and Bible-saturated?

LeAnne Hardy has provided us such a tool in her wonderful book, *Honey from the Comb, A guide to Focused Prayer Using Scripture.* Using the familiar ACTS—Adoration, Confession, Thanksgiving, and Supplication—Hardy provides nearly one hundred sub-theme categories for prayer. Her own words are of great practical use, but kept to a minimum so that we are led to pray in ways that are honoring to God, humbling to ourselves, filled with thankfulness, and then requests that keep us praying in the will of God. I see this book as showing us how to apply the balance of the traditional *Lord's Prayer* of Jesus to our expansion of that prayer for personal use. I commend this work to you, not as a book to read straight through, but as a tool, alongside your Bible, to strengthen your prayer experience, and thus your relationship with God.

—Tom Macy, Pastor of Shepherding, Faith Church, Indianapolis, Indiana

Introduction

Pandemic.
Economic disaster.
Social injustice.
Fighting in the streets.
Personal struggles with relationships,
health problems
and feelings of failure and inadequacy.

We live in stressful times. Like Peter with the waves of the storm crashing around him (Matthew 14:29-30), it is easy to focus on the problems instead of on the one who is able to calm the storm (Luke 8:24), knows the end from the beginning (Isaiah 46:10) and works all things for the good of those who love him (Romans 8:28).

This book is designed to help you to focus on who God is and what he is like as well as what he expects of you, his child, regardless of circumstances or what the storm throws at you.

Part 1, Adoration, collects verses of Scripture that describe our incredible God and his character.

Part 2, Confession, responds with passages for self-evaluation as you compare your own life to God's standards.

Part 3, Thanksgiving, directs your thoughts to passages where the Bible writers thank God for things that have their parallel in our own lives.

Part 4, Supplication, collects verses to help you focus on your own character, asking God to make you more like himself in a variety of areas.

This book does not contain prayers—words for you to say to God. It contains Scripture—God's words to you. As you read these words, I hope you will pray them back to God from the context of your life.

You may want to read through the verses on a specific topic to appreciate the flow of the language and beauty of the poetry, but be sure to return phrase by phrase to think about the meaning and make it your own. Under 'The Almighty' you will read,

Is anything too hard for the LORD? Genesis 18:14a

You might then pray something like this: "No, Lord, I know that nothing is too hard for you, even this problem that I am facing today." When you read

He performs wonders that cannot be fathomed,
Job 9:10

you could say, "Lord, I have seen the things you have already done in my life, wonderful things that I still don't understand, like how you brought me to yourself and what you are doing to make me more like you." The verse continues

miracles that cannot be counted.

You may tell the Lord, "I can't even count the marvelous things you have done for me," then list some specific things you have seen him do that remind you of his mighty power. Continue through the verses on that topic, praying them back to the Lord in the context of your present situation. Formatting is designed to help you focus phrase by phrase.

There is no rule that says you have to read this book in order or do all the parts every day. If you are feeling discouraged or facing a crisis, you might want to spend more time on Adoration, focusing on God rather than circumstances. If you are struggling with something in your life, you may need to flip to the pages in Part 3 that talk about relevant character traits. You may choose to use the lists in Part 2, Confession, weekly instead of daily.

This collection is not intended to take the place of regular reading and study of the whole Word of God. Nor is it a book of theology; passages have been chosen for their worship quality, not for their contribution to a study of doctrine. I would encourage you to look up the context of the verses in your own Bible. The margins are wide so that you will have room to add other verses that are meaningful to you.

You might consider buying the electronic version as well so you will always have these verses with you for a spontaneous prayer retreat while hiking, standing in line or waiting in a doctor's office.

As the Apostle Paul prayed for the believers in the Turkish city of Ephesus, so I pray

> that out of his glorious riches [God] may strengthen you with power through his Spirit in your inner being, so that Christ may dwell in your hearts through faith. Ephesians 3:16

Sincerely,
LeAnne Hardy

Part I
Adoration

Adoration

Adoration is praising God for who he is and what he is like. It focuses on his character more than on the specifics of what he has done. (We'll get to that in the Thanksgiving section.) The following passages are chosen to help you meditate on different aspects of this great God of ours.

The Almighty

Whether it is removing a dictator or changing the heart of a difficult boss, healing a dreaded disease or giving you the strength to live with the pain, there is nothing too difficult for our God. As you meditate on these verses, praise him for the ways in which you see his power that raised Christ from the dead at work in your life today.

Is anything too hard for the LORD? Genesis 18:14a

He performs wonders that cannot be fathomed,
    miracles that cannot be counted. Job 9:10

Who has gone up to heaven and come down?
    Whose hands have gathered up the wind?
Who has wrapped up the waters in his cloak?
    Who has established all the ends of the earth?
What is his name, and the name of his son?
    Tell me if you know! Proverbs 30:4

Your right hand, LORD,
    was majestic in power.
Your right hand, LORD,
    shattered the enemy. Exodus 15:6a

Yours, LORD, is the greatness and the power
    and the glory and the majesty and the splendor,
for everything in heaven and earth is yours.
1 Chronicles 29:11

No one is like you, LORD;
    you are great,
    and your name is mighty in power. Jeremiah 10:6

Adoration

The LORD does whatever pleases him,
   in the heavens and on the earth,
   in the seas and all their depths. Psalm 135:6

Ah, Sovereign LORD, you have made the heavens and the earth by your great power and outstretched arm. Nothing is too hard for you. Jeremiah 32:17

He made the earth by his power;
   he founded the world by his wisdom
   and stretched out the heavens by his understanding.
When he thunders, the waters in the heavens roar;
   he makes clouds rise from the ends of the earth.
He sends lightning with the rain
   and brings out the wind from his storehouses.
   Jeremiah 51:15-16

We eagerly await a Savior from [heaven], the Lord Jesus Christ, who, by the power that enables him to bring everything under his control, will transform our lowly bodies so that they will be like his glorious body. Philippians 3.20b-21

Jesus looked at them and said, "With man this is impossible, but with God all things are possible." Matthew 19:26

[His] power is the same as the mighty strength he exerted when he raised Christ from the dead. Ephesians 1:19b-20a

After this I heard what sounded like the roar of a great multitude in heaven shouting: "Hallelujah! Salvation and glory and power belong to our God." Revelation 19:1

The Comforter

The God who experienced rejection when he walked this earth, wept at the grave of a friend, and died a painful death, knows how to comfort his children in all situations. He has sent his Holy Spirit to live in us so we will not feel abandoned like orphans, but reach out with his comfort to others. As you read these verses, rest in that comfort, and praise the One who is able to comfort those you know who need to experience it today.

> He heals the brokenhearted
> > and binds up their wounds. Psalm 147:3
>
> The LORD is close to the brokenhearted
> > and saves those who are crushed in spirit.
> > Psalm 34:18
>
> A father to the fatherless, a defender of widows,
> > is God in his holy dwelling.
>
> God sets the lonely in families,
> > he leads forth the prisoners with singing; Psalm 68:5-6b
>
> In all their distress he too was distressed,
> > and the angel of his presence saved them.
>
> In his love and mercy he redeemed them;
> > he lifted them up and carried them
> > all the days of old. Isaiah 63:9
>
> My God, my God,
> > why have you forsaken me?
>
> Why are you so far from saving me,
> > so far from the words of my groaning?

Adoration

I will declare your name to my people;
    in the congregation I will praise you.
You who fear the LORD, praise him!
    All you descendants of Jacob, honor him!
Revere him, all you descendants of Israel!

For he has not despised or disdained
    the suffering of the afflicted one;
he has not hidden his face from him
    but has listened to his cry for help. Psalm 22:1, 22-24

I waited patiently for the LORD;
    he turned to me and heard my cry.
He lifted me out of the slimy pit,
    out of the mud and mire;
he set my feet on a rock
    and gave me a firm place to stand.
He put a new song in my mouth,
    a hymn of praise to our God.
Many will see and fear the LORD
    and put their trust in him. Psalm 40:1-3

Though you have made me see troubles,
    many and bitter,
    you will restore my life again;
from the depths of the earth
    you will again bring me up.
You will increase my honor
    and comfort me once more. Psalm 71:20-21

    I will ask the Father, and he will give you another advocate to help you and be with you forever—the Spirit of truth. The world cannot accept him, because it neither sees him nor knows him. But you know him, for he lives with you and will be in you. I will not leave you as orphans; I will come to you. John 14:16-18

Honey from the Comb

Praise be to the God and Father of our Lord Jesus Christ, the Father of compassion and the God of all comfort, who comforts us in all our troubles, so that we can comfort those in any trouble with the comfort we ourselves have received from God. For just as we share abundantly in the sufferings of Christ, so also our comfort abounds through Christ. 2 Corinthians 1:3-5

The Covenant Maker

In the Old Testament God made covenants (or contracts) with Noah, Abraham, David and others. He makes a new covenant with us to bring us into his family even if we aren't physically descended from Abraham, and he writes that covenant on our hearts. We renew this contract every time we take the Lord's Supper. As you meditate on these verses, praise God for making you his legal partner; he is never guilty of breach of contract.

> Know therefore that the LORD your God is God; he is the faithful God, keeping his covenant of love to a thousand generations of those who love him and keep his commands. Deuteronomy 7:9

> I will make a covenant of peace with them; it will be an everlasting covenant ... I will be their God, and they will be my people. Ezekiel 37:26a, 27b

> "Though the mountains be shaken
>   and the hills be removed,
> yet my unfailing love for you will not be shaken
>   nor my covenant of peace be removed,"
>   says the LORD, who has compassion on you.
> Isaiah 54:10

> If you can break my covenant with the day and my covenant with the night, so that day and night no longer come at their appointed time, then my covenant...can be broken and David will no longer have a descendant to reign on his throne. Jeremiah 33:20-21

"The days are coming," declares the LORD,
    "when I will make a new covenant
        with the house of Israel
    and with the house of Judah....
"This is the covenant I will make with the house of Israel
    after that time," declares the LORD.
"I will put my law in their minds
    and write it on their hearts.
I will be their God,
    and they will be my people.
No longer will they teach their neighbor,
    or a man his brother, saying, `Know the LORD,'
because they will all know me,
    from the least of them to the greatest,"
    declares the LORD.
"For I will forgive their wickedness
    and will remember their sins no more."
    Jeremiah 31:31, 33-34

"The Lord has sworn
    and will not change his mind:
        `You are a priest forever.' "
Because of this oath, Jesus has become the guarantor of a better covenant. Hebrews 7:21b-22

    After the supper [Jesus] took the cup, saying, "This cup is the new covenant in my blood, which is poured out for you." Luke 22:20

    Now may the God of peace, who through the blood of the eternal covenant brought back from the dead our Lord Jesus, that great Shepherd of the sheep, equip you with everything good for doing his will, and may he work in us what is pleasing to him, through Jesus Christ, to whom be glory for ever and ever. Amen. Hebrews 13:20-21

The Creator

Whether God formed the world instantly in six days or patiently over six eons of time, he brought it all into being for his own pleasure, and it was good. As you read these verses, praise the one who imagined and created everything from warthogs to majestic sequoias, from your own DNA to galaxies of stars.

> Do you not know? Have you not heard?
>   The LORD is the everlasting God,
> the Creator of the ends of the earth. Isaiah 40:28

> In the beginning God created the heavens and the earth. Genesis 1:1

> Then God said, "Let us make mankind in our image, in our likeness, so that they may rule over the fish in the sea and the birds in the sky, over the livestock and all the wild animals, and over all the creatures that move along the ground."

> So God created mankind in his own image,
>   in the image of God he created them;
> male and female he created them. Genesis 1:26-27

> God saw all that he had made, and it was very good. And there was evening, and there was morning—the sixth day.
>   Thus the heavens and the earth were completed in all their vast array. Genesis 1:31-2:1

Where were you when I laid the earth's foundation?

Tell me, if you understand.
Who marked off its dimensions? Surely you know!
   Who stretched a measuring line across it?
On what were its footings set,
   or who laid its cornerstone—
while the morning stars sang together
   and all the angels shouted for joy? Job 38:4-7

Stand up and praise the LORD your God, who is from everlasting to everlasting.

Blessed be your glorious name, and may it be exalted above all blessing and praise. You alone are the LORD. You made the heavens, even the highest heavens, and all their starry host, the earth and all that is on it, the seas and all that is in them. You give life to everything, and the multitudes of heaven worship you. Nehemiah 9:5b-6

The heavens declare the glory of God;
   the skies proclaim the work of his hands. Psalm 19:1

Through him all things were made; without him nothing was made that has been made. John 1:3

The God who made the world and everything in it is the Lord of heaven and earth and does not live in temples built by human hands. Acts 17:24

For you created my inmost being;
   you knit me together in my mother's womb.
I praise you because I am fearfully
   and wonderfully made;
your works are wonderful,
   I know that full well. Psalm 139:13-14

Adoration

This is what the LORD says:
"Heaven is my throne,
    and the earth is my footstool.
Where is the house you will build for me?
    Where will my resting place be?
Has not my hand made all these things,
    and so they came into being?"
    declares the LORD. Isaiah 66:1-2a

Eternal God

There has never been a time when God was not, and there will never be a time when he stops existing. He is outside our time and space; his nature and character are unchanged by it. Praise the God who simply is.

I AM who I AM. Exodus 3:14

Lord, you have been our dwelling place
    throughout all generations.
Before the mountains were born
    or you brought forth the whole world,
    from everlasting to everlasting, you are God.
Psalm 90:1-2

For since the creation of the world God's invisible qualities—his eternal power and divine nature—have been clearly seen, being understood from what has been made, so that people are without excuse. Romans 1:20

You remain the same,
    and your years will never end. Psalm 102:27

Your throne was established long ago;
    you are from all eternity…
Your statutes, LORD, stand firm;
    holiness adorns your house
    for endless days. Psalm 93:2, 5

Do you not know?
    Have you not heard?
The LORD is the everlasting God,

Adoration

    the Creator of the ends of the earth.
He will not grow tired or weary,
    and his understanding no one can fathom.
<small>Isaiah 40:28</small>

In my vision at night I looked, and there before me was one like a son of man, coming with the clouds of heaven. He approached the Ancient of Days and was led into his presence. He was given authority, glory and sovereign power; all peoples, nations and peoples of every language worshiped him. His dominion is an everlasting dominion that will not pass away, and his kingdom is one that will never be destroyed.
<small>Daniel 7:13-14</small>

But do not forget this one thing, dear friends: With the Lord a day is like a thousand years, and a thousand years are like a day. <small>2 Peter 3:8</small>

"I am the Alpha and the Omega," says the Lord God, "who is, and who was, and who is to come, the Almighty." <small>Revelation 1:8</small>

Whenever the living creatures give glory, honor and thanks to him who sits on the throne and who lives for ever and ever, the twenty-four elders fall down before him who sits on the throne, and worship him who lives for ever and ever. <small>Revelation 4:9-10a</small>

Now to the King eternal, immortal, invisible, the only God, be honor and glory for ever and ever. Amen. <small>1 Timothy 1:17</small>

Our Father

God compares himself to a parent who tenderly cares for his child even when that child refuses to be grateful. As you pray these verses, consider how your compassionate father may be pushing you into uncomfortable situations so you will learn to fly and grow up into the inheritance he has prepared for you.

> I will be a Father to you,
>   and you will be my sons and daughters,
> says the Lord Almighty." 2 Corinthians 6:18

> I am Israel's father,
>   and Ephraim is my firstborn son. Jeremiah 31:9c

> It was I who taught Ephraim to walk,
>   taking them by the arms;
> but they did not realize
>   it was I who healed them.
> I led them with cords of human kindness,
>   with ties of love.
> To them I was like one who lifts
>   a little child to the cheek,
>   and I bent down to feed them. Hosea 11:3-4

> [The Lord] shielded him and cared for him;
>   he guarded him as the apple of his eye,
> like an eagle that stirs up its nest
>   and hovers over its young,
> that spreads its wings to catch them
>   and carries them aloft. Deuteronomy 32:10b-11

Adoration

As a father has compassion on his children,
    so the Lord has compassion on those who fear him;
for he knows how we are formed,
    he remembers that we are dust. Psalm 103:13-14

As a mother comforts her child,
    so will I comfort you. Isaiah 66:13a

Can a mother forget the baby at her breast
    and have no compassion
    on the child she has borne?
Though she may forget,
    I will not forget you! Isaiah 49:15

    See what great love the Father has lavished on us, that we should be called children of God! 1 John 3:1a

    Because you are his sons, God sent the Spirit of his Son into our hearts, the Spirit who calls out, "Abba, Father." So you are no longer a slave, but God's child; and since you are his child, God has made you also an heir. Galatians 4:6-7

    The Spirit you received brought about your adoption to sonship. And by him we cry, "Abba, Father." The Spirit himself testifies with our spirit that we are God's children. Now if we are children, then we are heirs—heirs of God and co-heirs with Christ, if indeed we share in his sufferings in order that we may also share in his glory. Romans 8:15b-17

Our Father in heaven,
    hallowed be your name,
your kingdom come,
your will be done,
    on earth as it is in heaven. Matthew 6:9-13

Faithful Promise Keeper

God keeps his promise to grandparents, parents and children. Nothing can make him change his mind about saving you if you have given your life to him. As you read these verses, praise him for the promises you have seen him keep in your own life.

Praise the LORD, all you nations;
    extol him, all you peoples.
For great is his love toward us,
    and the faithfulness of the LORD endures forever.
Praise the LORD. Psalm 117

Not to us, LORD, not to us
    but to your name be the glory,
because of your love and faithfulness. Psalm 115:1

Your love, LORD, reaches to the heavens,
    your faithfulness to the skies. Psalm 36:5

The LORD is trustworthy in all he promises
    and faithful in all he does. Psalm 145:13b

The works of his hands are faithful and just;
    All his precepts are trustworthy.
They are established for ever and ever,
    enacted in faithfulness and uprightness. Psalm 111:7-8

"For I know the plans I have for you," declares the LORD, "plans to prosper you and not to harm you, plans to give you hope and a future. Jeremiah 29:11

Adoration

He who began a good work in you will carry it on to completion until the day of Christ Jesus. Philippians 1:6

Because of the LORD's great love we are not consumed,
>   for his compassions never fail.
They are new every morning;
>   great is your faithfulness. Lamentations 3:22-23

Knowledge of the truth that leads to godliness [rests on] the hope of eternal life, which God, who does not lie, promised before the beginning of time. Titus 1:1-2

If we confess our sins, he is faithful and just and will forgive us our sins and purify us from all unrighteousness. 1 John 1:9

What if some were unfaithful? Will their unfaithfulness nullify God's faithfulness? Not at all! Let God be true, and every human being a liar. Romans 3:3-4a

If we are faithless,
>   he remains faithful,
>   for he cannot disown himself. 2 Timothy 2:13

No matter how many promises God has made, they are "Yes" in Christ. And so through him the "Amen" is spoken by us to the glory of God. 2 Corinthians 1:20

Let us hold unswervingly to the hope we profess, for he who promised is faithful. Hebrews 10:23

The Firstborn

Jesus is the first-born, not in the sense of having a beginning, but in the sense of the rights and responsibilities that a first-born son had in ancient cultures. Deuteronomy 21:17 calls the firstborn "the first sign of his father's strength." As you read, praise the Son who shows us the Father and has responsibility and authority both for the physical creation that he made and for the new creation of God's family.

> I will appoint him to be my firstborn
> > the most exalted of the kings of the earth.
> > Psalm 89:27
>
> When God brings his firstborn into the world, he says, "Let all God's angels worship him."
> Hebrews 1:6
>
> For those God foreknew he also predestined to be conformed to the likeness of his Son, that he might be the firstborn among many brothers and sisters. Romans 8:29

The Son is the image of the invisible God,
    the firstborn over all creation.
For in him all things were created:
    things in heaven and on earth,
        visible and invisible,
            whether thrones
                or powers
                    or rulers
                        or authorities;
all things have been created through him and for him.

Adoration

He is before all things,
    and in him all things hold together.
And he is the head of the body,
    the church;
he is the beginning
    and the firstborn from among the dead,
so that in everything he might have the supremacy.

For God was pleased to have all his fullness
    dwell in him,
and through him to reconcile to himself all things,
    whether things on earth
        or things in heaven,
by making peace through his blood,
    shed on the cross. Colossians 1:15-20

    If Christ has not been raised, your faith is futile; you are still in your sins…But Christ has indeed been raised from the dead, the firstfruits of those who have fallen asleep. 1 Corinthians 15:17, 20

    Jesus Christ…is the faithful witness, the firstborn from the dead, and the ruler of the kings of the earth.
    To him who loves us and has freed us from our sins by his blood, and has made us to be a kingdom and priests to serve his God and Father—to him be glory and power for ever and ever! Amen. Revelation 1:5-6

Generous Provider

As great as God is, he reaches out to us generously and meets our needs beyond our imagining. As you meditate on these verses, thank him for his generosity to you and open your mouth like an infant to be filled.

I am the LORD your God,
>who brought you up out of Egypt.
Open wide your mouth and I will fill it. Psalm 81:10

Wealth and honor come from you;
>you are the ruler of all things.
In your hands are strength and power
>to exalt and give strength to all. 1 Chronicles 29:12

How abundant are the good things
>that you have stored up for those who fear you,
that you bestow in the sight of all,
>on those who take refuge in you. Psalm 31:19

The lions may grow weak and hungry,
>but those who seek the LORD lack no good thing.
>Psalm 34:10

For the LORD God is a sun and shield;
>the LORD bestows favor and honor;
no good thing does he withhold
>from those whose walk is blameless. Psalm 84:11

Thanks be to God for his indescribable gift!
>2 Corinthians 9:15

Adoration

He who did not spare his own Son, but gave him up for us all—how will he not also, along with him, graciously give us all things? Romans 8:32

But seek first his kingdom and his righteousness, and all these things will be given to you as well. Matthew 6: 33

And my God will meet all your needs according to the riches of his glory in Christ Jesus. Philippians 4:19

If you remain in me and my words remain in you, ask whatever you wish, and it will be done for you. John 15:7

Ask and it will be given to you; seek and you will find; knock and the door will be opened to you. For everyone who asks receives; he who seeks finds; and to him who knocks, the door will be opened. Which of you, if your son asks for bread, will give him a stone? Or if he asks for a fish, will give him a snake? If you, then, though you are evil, know how to give good gifts to your children, how much more will your Father in heaven give good gifts to those who ask him! Matthew 7:7-11

What no eye has seen,
    what no ear has heard,
and what no human mind has conceived—
    the things God has prepared
    for those who love him—
these are the things God has revealed to us
    by his Spirit. 1 Corinthians 2:9 -10a

Honey from the Comb

For you know the grace of our Lord Jesus Christ, that though he was rich, yet for your sakes he became poor, so that you through his poverty might become rich. 2 Corinthians 8:9

Now to him who is able to do immeasurably more than all we ask or imagine, according to his power that is at work within us, to him be glory in the church and in Christ Jesus throughout all generations, for ever and ever! Amen. Ephesians 3:20-21

The Glorious One

Jesus is the 'friend of sinners' who brings us near the Father, but we must not forget that he is also King of kings and Lord of lords, the Holy One whose glory fills the temple. As you read these verses, praise God for his awesome glory seen in Father, Son and Holy Spirit.

> The heavens declare the glory of God;
>> the skies proclaim the work of his hands. Psalm 19:1

> Ascribe to the LORD, you heavenly beings,
>> ascribe to the LORD glory and strength.
>
> Ascribe to the LORD the glory due his name;
>> worship the LORD in the splendor of his holiness.
>
> The voice of the LORD is over the waters;
>> the God of glory thunders,
>> the Lord thunders over the mighty waters…
>
> The voice of the LORD twists the oaks
>> and strips the forests bare.
>
> And in his temple all cry, "Glory!" Psalm 29:1-3, 9

> In the year that King Uzziah died, [Isaiah] saw the Lord, high and exalted, seated on a throne, and the train of his robe filled the temple. Above him were seraphim, each with six wings: With two wings they covered their faces, with two they covered their feet, and with two they were flying. And they were calling to one another:
>> Holy, holy, holy is the LORD Almighty;
>> the whole earth is full of his glory."
>
> At the sound of their voices the doorposts and thresholds shook and the temple was filled with smoke. Isaiah 6:1-4

We have seen his glory, the glory of the one and only Son, who came from the Father, full of grace and truth. John 1:14b

As [Jesus] was praying, the appearance of his face changed, and his clothes became as bright as a flash of lightning ... A cloud appeared and covered them, and they were afraid as they entered the cloud. A voice came from the cloud, saying, "This is my Son, whom I have chosen; listen to him." Luke 9:29, 34-35

When [Judas] was gone, Jesus said, "Now the Son of Man is glorified and God is glorified in him. If God is glorified in him, God will glorify the Son in himself, and will glorify him at once." John 13:31-32

Among the lampstands was someone like a son of man, dressed in a robe reaching down to his feet and with a golden sash around his chest. The hair on his head was white like wool, as white as snow, and his eyes were like blazing fire. His feet were like bronze glowing in a furnace, and his voice was like the sound of rushing waters. In his right hand he held seven stars, and coming out of his mouth was a sharp double-edged sword. His face was like the sun shining in all its brilliance.
When I saw him, I fell at his feet as though dead. Then he placed his right hand on me and said: "Do not be afraid. I am the First and the Last. I am the Living One; I was dead, and behold I am alive for ever and ever! And I hold the keys of death and Hades. Revelation 1:13-18

Goodness Itself

God's goodness is his nature. It is also what he does. When we call something 'good' we are talking about how much it is like what God does. Praise him for his goodness to you personally.

> Good and upright is the LORD;
>   therefore he instructs sinners in his ways.
> He guides the humble in what is right
>   and teaches them his way.
> All the ways of the LORD are loving and faithful
>   toward those who keep the demands
>   of his covenant. Psalm 25:8-10

> For the LORD is good and his love endures forever;
>   his faithfulness continues through all generations.
>   Psalm 100:5

> Give thanks to the LORD, for he is good;
>   his love endures forever.
> Let the redeemed of the LORD tell their story—
>   those he redeemed from the hand of the foe,
> those he gathered from the lands,
>   from east and west, from north and south.
> Let them give thanks to the LORD for his unfailing love
>   and his wonderful deeds for men. Psalm 107:1-3, 8

> The LORD is gracious and compassionate,
>   slow to anger and rich in love.
> The LORD is good to all;
>   he has compassion on all he has made.
>   Psalm 145:8-9

Yet he has not left himself without testimony: He has shown kindness by giving you rain from heaven and crops in their seasons; he provides you with plenty of food and fills your hearts with joy. Acts 14:17

He causes his sun to rise on the evil and the good, and sends rain on the righteous and the unrighteous. Matthew 5:45b

"Which of you, if his son asks for bread, will give him a stone? Or if he asks for a fish, will give him a snake? If you, then, though you are evil, know how to give good gifts to your children, how much more will your Father in heaven give good gifts to those who ask him! Matthew 7:9-11

Taste and see that the LORD is good. Psalm 34:8a

The LORD is good to those whose hope is in him,
    to the one who seeks him; Lamentations 3:25

Gracious God

Grace is another word for generosity. It means getting more than we deserve. Grace isn't based on anything wonderful in us, nor is it something God owes us. God not only saved us and brought us into his family when we didn't deserve it, but his grace restrains evil and holds us when we are weak. As you meditate on these verses, praise God for the grace you have seen in your life.

> The LORD did not set his affection on you and choose you because you were more numerous than other peoples, for you were the fewest of all peoples. But it was because the LORD loved you and kept the oath he swore to your forefathers that he brought you out with a mighty hand and redeemed you from the land of slavery, from the power of Pharaoh king of Egypt. Deuteronomy 7:7-8

> And God raised us up with Christ and seated us with him in the heavenly realms in Christ Jesus, in order that in the coming ages he might show the incomparable riches of his grace, expressed in his kindness to us in Christ Jesus.
> For it is by grace you have been saved, through faith—and this is not from yourselves, it is the gift of God—not by works, so that no one can boast. Ephesians 2:6-9

> For the grace of God has appeared that offers salvation to all people. Titus 2:11

But when the kindness and love of God our Savior appeared, he saved us, not because of righteous things we had done, but because of his mercy. He saved us through the washing of rebirth and renewal by the Holy Spirit, whom he poured out on us generously through Jesus Christ our Savior, so that, having been justified by his grace, we might become heirs having the hope of eternal life. Titus 3:4-7

What then shall we say? Is God unjust? Not at all! For he says to Moses,

> "I will have mercy on whom I have mercy,
>   and I will have compassion on whom I
>   have compassion."

It does not, therefore, depend on man's desire or effort, but on God's mercy. Romans 9:14-16

[The Lord] said to me, "My grace is sufficient for you, for my power is made perfect in weakness." Therefore I will boast all the more gladly about my weaknesses, so that Christ's power may rest on me. 2 Corinthians 12: 9

God is able to bless you abundantly, so that in all things at all times, having all that you need, you will abound in every good work. 2 Corinthians 9:8

Our Great High Priest

The Old Testament is full of pictures of what the Messiah would be like. Jesus is a shepherd. He is the sacrificial Lamb. He is also the Priest who offers the perfect sacrifice for sin. He intercedes for us like a Lawyer going before the Judge on our behalf. As you think on these verses, praise him because in his humanity he understands our weaknesses, but as God he is not limited by them.

> Therefore, since we have a great high priest who has ascended into heaven, Jesus the Son of God, let us hold firmly to the faith we profess. For we do not have a high priest who is unable to sympathize with our weaknesses, but we have one who has been tempted in every way, just as we are—yet was without sin. Let us then approach the throne of grace with confidence, so that we may receive mercy and find grace to help us in our time of need. Hebrews 4:14-16

> Every high priest is selected from among the people and is appointed to represent the people in matters related to God, to offer gifts and sacrifices for sins. He is able to deal gently with those who are ignorant and are going astray, since he himself is subject to weakness. This is why he has to offer sacrifices for his own sins, as well as for the sins of the people. Hebrews 5:1-3

> Now there have been many [human] priests, since death prevented them from continuing in office; but because Jesus lives forever, he has a permanent priesthood. Therefore he is able to

save completely those who come to God through him, because he always lives to intercede for them.

Such a high priest truly meets our need—
one who is holy,
   blameless,
      pure,
         set apart from sinners,
            exalted above the heavens.
Unlike the other high priests, he does not need to offer sacrifices day after day, first for his own sins, and then for the sins of the people. He sacrificed for their sins once for all when he offered himself. For the law appoints as high priests men in all their weakness; but the oath, which came after the law, appointed the Son, who has been made perfect forever. Hebrews 7:23-28

We have this hope as an anchor for the soul, firm and secure. It enters the inner sanctuary behind the curtain, where our forerunner Jesus, has entered on our behalf. He has become a high priest forever, in the order of Melchizedek. Hebrews 6.19-20

Now the main point of what we are saying is this: We do have such a high priest, who sat down at the right hand of the throne of the Majesty in heaven, and who serves in the sanctuary, the true tabernacle set up by the Lord, not by a mere human being. Hebrews 8:1-2

My dear children, I write this to you so that you will not sin. But if anybody does sin, we have an advocate with the Father—Jesus Christ, the Righteous One. 1 John 2:1

The Holy One of Israel

'Holy' means separated from the world and unpolluted by it. It has the idea of being untouched by any imperfection. All the Old Testament ritual laws were meant to show God's people how utterly different God is from themselves and the ordinary everyday world around them. As you meditate on these verses, acknowledge to God his unique perfection.

"Do not come any closer," God said. "Take off your sandals, for the place where you are standing is holy ground." Exodus 3:5

Who among the gods is like you, LORD?
    Who is like you—
majestic in holiness,
    awesome in glory,
    working wonders? Exodus 15:11

[The seraphim] were calling to one another:
    "Holy, holy, holy is the LORD Almighty;
the whole earth is full of his glory." Isaiah 6:3

Exalt the LORD our God
    and worship at his holy mountain,
    for the LORD our God is holy. Psalm 99:9

For this is what the high and lofty One says—
    he who lives forever, whose name is holy:
"I live in a high and holy place,
    but also with him who is contrite and lowly in spirit,
to revive the spirit of the lowly
    and to revive the heart of the contrite. Isaiah 57:15

This is the message we have heard from him and declare to you: God is light; in him there is no darkness at all. 1 John 1:5

Who will not fear you, Lord,
    and bring glory to your name?
For you alone are holy. Revelation 15:4a

Worship the Lord in the splendor of his holiness. 1 Chronicles 16:29c

Holy, holy, holy
    is the Lord God Almighty,
who was, and is, and is to come. Revelation 4:8

Hope of the Nations

Although God chose the family of Abraham to prepare the way for his coming, it was always his plan to reconcile the whole world to himself. Praise God with Slovaks, Zulus, Guarani, Hmong and believers of every other nation.

> The LORD reigns,
>   let the nations tremble;
> he sits enthroned between the cherubim,
>   let the earth shake.
> Great is the LORD in Zion;
>   he is exalted over all the nations. Psalm 99:1-2

> [The Lord] says:
> "It is too small a thing for you to be my servant
>   to restore the tribes of Jacob
>   and bring back those of Israel I have kept.
> I will also make you a light for the Gentiles,
>   that you may bring my salvation
>   to the ends of the earth...
> See, they will come from afar—
>   some from the north, some from the west,
>   some from the region of Aswan. " Isaiah 49:6, 12

> Many peoples will come and say,
>   "Come, let us go up to the mountain of the LORD,
>   to the house of the God of Jacob.
> He will teach us his ways,
>   so that we may walk in his paths." Isaiah 2:3-4a

And in that day a great trumpet will sound. Those who were perishing in Assyria and those who were exiled in Egypt will come and worship the LORD on the holy mountain in Jerusalem.
Isaiah 27:13

My house will be called a house of prayer for all nations. Isaiah 56:7c

Here is my servant whom I have chosen,
   the one I love, in whom I delight;
I will put my Spirit on him,
   and he will proclaim justice to the nations.…
In his name the nations will put their hope.
Matthew 12:18, 21

"My name will be great among the nations, from where the sun rises to where it sets. In every place incense and pure offerings will be brought to me, because my name will be great among the nations," says the LORD Almighty.
Malachi 1:11

I say to you that many will come from the east and the west, and will take their places at the feast with Abraham, Isaac and Jacob in the kingdom of heaven. Matthew 8:11

And this gospel of the kingdom will be preached in the whole world as a testimony to all nations, and then the end will come. Matthew 24:14

Clap your hands, all you nations;
   shout to God with cries of joy.
For the LORD Most High is awesome,
   the great King over all the earth.

Adoration

For God is the King of all the earth;
    sing to him a psalm of praise.
God reigns over the nations;
    God is seated on his holy throne.
The nobles of the nations assemble
    as the people of the God of Abraham,
for the kings of the earth belong to God;
    he is greatly exalted. Psalm 47:1-2, 7-9

Humble Servant

The God of all the universe did not cling to who he was as God. He chose to be born as a helpless baby in a working-class family in a subject nation of the Roman Empire so that he could die a criminal's death to pay for our sin. As you read these verses, bow your heart in the presence of this humble Jesus and call him Lord.

> Foxes have dens and birds have nests, but the Son of Man has no place to lay his head. Matthew 8:20

> For even the Son of Man did not come to be served, but to serve, and to give his life as a ransom for many. Mark 10:45

> It was just before the Passover Festival. Jesus knew that the hour had come for him to leave this world and go to the Father. Having loved his own who were in the world, he loved them to the end.
> The evening meal was in progress, and the devil had already prompted Judas, the son of Simon Iscariot, to betray Jesus. Jesus knew that the Father had put all things under his power, and that he had come from God and was returning to God; so he got up from the meal, took off his outer clothing, and wrapped a towel around his waist. After that, he poured water into a basin and began to wash his disciples' feet, drying them with the towel that was wrapped around him. John 13:1-5

Adoration

In your relationships with one another, have the same mindset as Christ Jesus:
Who, being in very nature God,
    did not consider equality with God
    something to be used to his own advantage;
Rather, he made himself nothing,
    by taking the very nature of a servant,
    being made in human likeness.
And being found in appearance as a man,
    he humbled himself
By becoming obedient to death—
    even death on a cross!

Therefore God exalted him to the highest place
    and gave him the name that is above every name,
that at the name of Jesus every knee should bow,
    in heaven
        and on earth
            and under the earth,
and every tongue confess that Jesus Christ is Lord,
    to the glory of God the Father. Philippians 2:5-11

Immanuel, God with Us

Theologians talk about God being immanent. He surrounds us with his presence. He invites us to call him Father. He even became a human baby and walked in our world. As you read these verses, revel in God's presence and praise him because he hears our prayers, invites us to come to him and made it possible when he became one of us.

> My dwelling place will be with them; I will be their God, and they will be my people. Ezekiel 37:27

> What other nation is so great as to have their gods near them the way the LORD our God is near us whenever we pray to him? Deuteronomy 4:7

> When you pass through the waters,
>   I will be with you;
> and when you pass through the rivers,
>   they will not sweep over you.
> When you walk through the fire,
>   you will not be burned;
> the flames will not set you ablaze. Isaiah 43:2

> The Word became flesh and made his dwelling among us. We have seen his glory, the glory of the one and only Son, who came from the Father, full of grace and truth. John 1:14

> The virgin will be with child and will give birth to a son, and they will call him Immanuel (which means "God with us"). Matthew 1:23

For where two or three gather in my name, there am I with them." Matthew 18:20

But now in Christ Jesus you who once were far away have been brought near through the blood of Christ. Ephesians 2:13

In him and through faith in him we may approach God with freedom and confidence. Ephesians 3:12

Come near to God and he will come near to you. Wash your hands, you sinners, and purify your hearts, you double-minded. Grieve, mourn and wail. Change your laughter to mourning and your joy to gloom. Humble yourselves before the Lord, and he will lift you up. James 4:8-10

And I heard a loud voice from the throne saying, "Look! God's dwelling place is now among the people, and he will dwell with them. They will be his people, and God himself will be with them and be their God. Revelation 21:3

Just Judge

God is morally and legally right. He is never dishonest or unreasonable in his judgments. Praise him because he doesn't let us get away with sin, but calls it to our attention and punishes it so we will turn back to him. Invite him also to set right the injustices of the world.

> He is the Rock, his works are perfect,
> and all his ways are just.
> A faithful God who does no wrong,
> upright and just is he. Deuteronomy 32:4

> I will discipline you but only in due measure;
> I will not let you go entirely unpunished.
> Jeremiah 46:28d

> The crucible for silver and the furnace for gold,
> but the LORD tests the heart. Proverbs 17:3

> The Lord will reward each one for whatever good they do, whether they are slave or free. Ephesians 6:8

> If you say, "But we knew nothing about this,"
> does not he who weighs the heart perceive it?
> Does not he who guards your life know it?
> Will he not repay everyone
> according to what they have done? Proverbs 24:12

> Woe to the city of oppressors,
> rebellious and defiled!…
> The LORD within her is righteous;

Adoration

he does no wrong.
Morning by morning he dispenses his justice,
    and every new day he does not fail,
yet the unrighteous know no shame. Zephaniah 3:1, 5

Great and marvelous are your deeds,
    Lord God Almighty.
Just and true are your ways,
    King of the nations. Revelation 15:3b

You are just in these judgments, O Holy One,
    you who are and who were; Revelation 16:5b

Let the rivers clap their hands,
    let the mountains sing together for joy;
let them sing before the LORD,
    for he comes to judge the earth.
He will judge the world in righteousness
    and the peoples with equity. Psalm 98:8-9

The LORD works righteousness
    and justice for all the oppressed. Psalm 103:6

The LORD longs to be gracious to you;
    therefore he will rise up to show you compassion.
For the LORD is a God of justice.
    Blessed are all who wait for him! Isaiah 30:18

    Then I saw a great white throne and him who was seated on it. The earth and the heavens fled from his presence, and there was no place for them. And I saw the dead, great and small, standing before the throne, and books were opened. Another book was opened, which is the book of life. The dead were judged according to what they had done as recorded in the books.

Honey from the Comb

The sea gave up the dead that were in it, and death and Hades gave up the dead that were in them, and each person was judged according to what they had done. Then death and Hades were thrown into the lake of fire. The lake of fire is the second death. Anyone whose name was not found written in the book of life was thrown into the lake of fire. Revelation 20:11-15

King of Kings

In the modern world we see kings either as figureheads or dictators, but God is a benevolent monarch over us, his people, and over all the rulers of the earth. As you meditate on these verses, picture yourself swearing allegiance to such a Lord, more perfect and eternal than all the kings of legend.

> Lift up your heads, you gates;
> > be lifted up, you ancient doors,
> > that the King of glory may come in.
>
> Who is this King of glory?
> > The LORD strong and mighty,
> > the LORD mighty in battle.
>
> Lift up your heads, you gates;
> > lift them up, you ancient doors,
> > that the King of glory may come in.
>
> Who is he, this King of glory?
> > The LORD Almighty—
> > he is the King of glory. Psalm 24:7-10

> The LORD reigns, he is robed in majesty;
> > the LORD is robed in majesty
> > and is armed with strength.
>
> Indeed, the world is firmly established;
> > it cannot be moved.
>
> Your throne was established long ago;
> > you are from all eternity. Psalm 93:1-2

> Come, let us sing for joy to the LORD;
> > let us shout aloud to the Rock of our salvation.
>
> Let us come before him with thanksgiving
> > and extol him with music and song.

Honey from the Comb

For the L<small>ORD</small> is the great God,
    the great King above all gods.
In his hand are the depths of the earth,
    and the mountain peaks belong to him.
The sea is his, for he made it,
    and his hands formed the dry land.
Come, let us bow down in worship,
    let us kneel before the L<small>ORD</small> our Maker;
    for he is our God
and we are the people of his pasture,
    the flock under his care. Psalm 95:1-7a

Clouds and thick darkness surround him;
    righteousness and justice are the foundation of his throne. Psalm 97:2

God, the blessed and only Ruler, the King of kings and Lord of lords, who alone is immortal and who lives in unapproachable light, whom no one has seen or can see. To him be honor and might forever. Amen. 1 Timothy 6:15b-16

The All-Knowing

God does not learn or grow in his knowledge as we do. It is part of who he is. He knows all about his creation and sees what is done in secret. As you read, tell him how glad you are for his intimate knowledge of you and your current situation.

> Oh, the depth of the riches of the wisdom and knowledge of God! How unsearchable his judgments, and his paths beyond tracing out! Romans 11:33

> Nothing in all creation is hidden from God's sight. Everything is uncovered and laid bare before the eyes of him to whom we must give account. Hebrews 4: 13

He determines the number of the stars
    and calls them each by name.
Great is our Lord and mighty in power;
    his understanding has no limit. Psalm 147:4-5

From heaven the LORD looks down
    and sees all mankind;
from his dwelling place he watches
    all who live on earth—
he who forms the hearts of all,
    who considers everything they do. Psalm 33:13-15

Before they call I will answer;
    while they are still speaking I will hear. Isaiah 65:24

But when you pray, go into your room, close the door and pray to your Father, who is unseen. Then your Father, who sees what is done in secret, will reward you. Matthew 6:6

God is greater than our hearts, and he knows everything. 1 John 3:20b

You have searched me, LORD
    and you know me.
You know when I sit and when I rise;
    you perceive my thoughts from afar.
You discern my going out and my lying down;
    you are familiar with all my ways.
Before a word is on my tongue
    You, LORD, know it completely...
My frame was not hidden from you
    when I was made in the secret place,
when I was woven together in the depths of the earth.
    Your eyes saw my unformed body;
All the days ordained for me
    were written in your book
    before one of them came to be. Psalm 139:1-4, 15-16

Lamb of God

Day after day Old Testament priests sacrificed bulls and goats to cover the sin of the people, but it was never enough. Those offerings were a picture of what God was planning to do—become flesh and offer his own blood to take away sin once and for all. As you read, join the angels of heaven in praising our sacrificial Lamb.

> The next day John saw Jesus coming toward him and said, "Look, the Lamb of God, who takes away the sin of the world! John 1:29

> For you know that it was not with perishable things such as silver or gold that you were redeemed from the empty way of life handed down to you from your ancestors, but with the precious blood of Christ, a lamb without blemish or defect. He was chosen before the creation of the world, but was revealed in these last times for your sake. Through him you believe in God, who raised him from the dead and glorified him, and so your faith and hope are in God. 1 Peter 1:18-21

> Then I saw a Lamb, looking as if it had been slain, standing in the center of the throne, encircled by the four living creatures and the elders...

> And they sang a new song:
>
> > "You are worthy to take the scroll
> > and to open its seals,

because you were slain,
    and with your blood you purchased for God
persons from every tribe
    and language
        and people
            and nation.

You have made them to be a kingdom
    and priests to serve our God,
and they will reign on the earth."

Then I looked and heard the voice of many angels, numbering thousands upon thousands, and ten thousand times ten thousand. They encircled the throne and the living creatures and the elders. In a loud voice they sang:

"Worthy is the Lamb, who was slain,
    to receive power
        and wealth
            and wisdom
                and strength
                      and honor
                          and glory
                              and praise!"

Then I heard every creature in heaven and on earth and under the earth and on the sea, and all that is in them, singing:

"To him who sits on the throne and to the Lamb be praise and honor and glory and power,
    for ever and ever!"

The four living creatures said, "Amen," and the elders fell down and worshiped. Revelation 5: 6a, 9-14

Source of Life

In our modern world of fast food and supermarkets, we forget how dependent the rest of the world is on the basics of bread and water. As you read and as you eat and drink today, praise Jesus who is the source of both physical and spiritual life.

> He is not served by human hands, as if he needed anything. Rather, he himself gives everyone life and breath and everything else... 'For in him we live and move and have our being.' Acts 17:25, 28

> In him was life, and that life was the light of all mankind. John 1:4

> Jesus answered, "Everyone who drinks this water will be thirsty again, but whoever drinks the water I give them will never thirst. Indeed, the water I give them will become in them a spring of water welling up to eternal life." John 4:13-14

> Jesus said to her, "I am the resurrection and the life. The one who believes in me will live, even though they die; and whoever lives by believing in me will never die." John 11:25-26a

> Jesus declared, "I am the bread of life. Whoever comes to me will never go hungry, and whoever believes in me will never be thirsty....
> "Your ancestors ate the manna in the desert, yet they died. But here is the bread that comes down from heaven, which anyone may eat and

not die. I am the living bread that came down from heaven. Whoever eats of this bread will live forever. This bread is my flesh, which I will give for the life of the world." John 6: 35, 49-51

I have come that they may have life, and have it to the full. John 10:10b

I am the vine; you are the branches. If you remain in me and I in you, you will bear much fruit; apart from me you can do nothing. John 15:5

I am the Living One; I was dead, and now look, I am alive for ever and ever! And I hold the keys of death and Hades. Revelation 1:18

I am the Alpha and the Omega, the Beginning and the End. To the thirsty I will give water without cost from the spring of the water of life. Revelation 21:6

Then the angel showed me the river of the water of life, as clear as crystal, flowing from the throne of God and of the Lamb down the middle of the great street of the city. On each side of the river stood the tree of life, bearing twelve crops of fruit, yielding its fruit every month. And the leaves of the tree are for the healing of the nations. Revelation 22:1-2

Come, all you who are thirsty,
   come to the waters;
and you who have no money,
   come, buy and eat!
Come, buy wine and milk
   without money and without cost.

Adoration

Why spend money on what is not bread,
    and your labor on what does not satisfy?
Listen, listen to me, and eat what is good,
    and you will delight in the richest of fare.
Give ear and come to me;
    listen, that you may live. Isaiah 55:1-2

Love

Before God created human beings, love existed in the Holy Trinity—Father, Son and Holy Spirit. Praise him because there is nothing that can separate you from that love—not physical hardships, spiritual powers or anything going on in your life right now or that might happen next week.

Because your love is better than life,
  my lips will glorify you.
I will praise you as long as I live,
  and in your name I will lift up my hands.
Psalm 63:3-4

The LORD appeared to us in the past, saying:
  "I have loved you with an everlasting love;
  I have drawn you with unfailing kindness.
Jeremiah 31:3

But God demonstrates his own love for us in this: While we were still sinners, Christ died for us. Romans 5:8

"For God so loved the world that he gave his one and only Son, that whoever believes in him shall not perish but have eternal life. John 3:16

Whoever does not love does not know God, because God is love. This is how God showed his love among us: He sent his one and only Son into the world that we might live through him. This is love: not that we loved God, but that he loved us and sent his Son as an atoning sacrifice for our sins. 1 John 4:8-10

Adoration

Who shall separate us from the love of Christ?
   Shall trouble
      or hardship
         or persecution
           or famine
              or nakedness
                 or danger
                    or sword?…
No, in all these things we are more than conquerors
   through him who loved us.
For I am convinced that neither death nor life,
   neither angels nor demons,
      neither the present nor the future,
         nor any powers,
           neither height nor depth,
              nor anything else in all creation,
will be able to separate us from the love of God
   that is in Christ Jesus our Lord. Romans 8: 35, 37-39

May our Lord Jesus Christ himself and God our Father, who loved us and by his grace gave us eternal encouragement and good hope, encourage your hearts and strengthen you in every good deed and word. 2 Thessalonians 2:16-17

Merciful Judge

If *grace* means giving us what we don't deserve, *mercy* means not giving us what we do deserve—punishment. God can show mercy and still be just because he has already paid the penalty for our sin on the cross. He does not stay angry and seek to get even for what we have done to him, but delights to show mercy. As you read these verses, tell God specific ways in which you have seen his mercy in your own life.

> And the Lord said, "I will cause all my goodness to pass in front of you, and I will proclaim my name, the Lord, in your presence. I will have mercy on whom I will have mercy, and I will have compassion on whom I will have compassion. Exodus 33:19b

> Lord, I have heard of your fame;
>   I stand in awe of your deeds, Lord.
> Renew them in our day,
>   in our time make them known;
>   in wrath remember mercy. Habakkuk 3:2

> Who is a God like you,
>   who pardons sin
>   and forgives the transgression
>   of the remnant of his inheritance?
> You do not stay angry forever
>   but delight to show mercy.
> You will again have compassion on us;
>   you will tread our sins underfoot
>   and hurl all our iniquities
>   into the depths of the sea. Micah 7:18-19

Adoration

His mercy extends to those who fear him,
    from generation to generation. Luke 1:50

The LORD is compassionate and gracious,
    slow to anger, abounding in love.
He will not always accuse,
    nor will he harbor his anger forever;
he does not treat us as our sins deserve
    or repay us according to our iniquities.
For as high as the heavens are above the earth,
    so great is his love for those who fear him;
as far as the east is from the west,
    so far has he removed our transgressions from us.
    Psalm 103:8-12

Praise be to the God and Father of our Lord Jesus Christ! In his great mercy he has given us new birth into a living hope through the resurrection of Jesus Christ from the dead, and into an inheritance that can never perish, spoil or fade. 1 Peter 1:3-4

Whoever conceals their sins does not prosper,
    but the one who confesses and renounces them
    finds mercy. Proverbs 28:13

Because of his great love for us, God, who is rich in mercy, made us alive with Christ even when we were dead in transgressions—it is by grace you have been saved. Ephesians 2:4-5

He saved us, not because of righteous things we had done, but because of his mercy. Titus 3:5a

The Only God

Many people today want to invent their own idea of what God is like, but that is exactly what they are—inventions. Although the gospel tells us to love and respect each person as created in God's image, we don't have to agree with their religious imaginations. As you meditate on these verses, give praise to the unique God of the Bible who became a man in Christ Jesus.

> See now that I myself am he!
>   There is no god besides me.
> I put to death and I bring to life,
>   I have wounded and I will heal,
>   and no one can deliver out of my hand.
> Deuteronomy 32:39

> "To whom will you compare me?
>   Or who is my equal?" says the Holy One.
> Isaiah 40:25

> I am the LORD; that is my name!
>   I will not yield my glory to another
>   or my praise to idols. Isaiah 42:8

> "You are my witnesses," declares the LORD,
>   "and my servant whom I have chosen,
> so that you may know and believe me
>   and understand that I am he.
> Before me no god was formed,
>   nor will there be one after me.
> I, even I, am the LORD,
>   and apart from me there is no savior.

Adoration

I have revealed and saved and proclaimed—
    I, and not some foreign god among you.
You are my witnesses," declares the LORD,
    "that I am God." Isaiah 43:10-12

This is what the LORD says—
    Israel's King and Redeemer, the LORD Almighty:
I am the first and I am the last;
    apart from me there is no God.
Who then is like me? Let him proclaim it. Isaiah 44:6-7a

There is no God apart from me,
a righteous God and a Savior;
    there is none but me. Isaiah 45:21b

Since ancient times no one has heard,
    no ear has perceived,
no eye has seen any God besides you,
    who acts on behalf of those who wait for him.
Isaiah 64:4

    There is but one God, the Father, from whom all things came and for whom we live; and there is but one Lord, Jesus Christ, through whom all things came and through whom we live. 1 Corinthians 8:6

    There is one God and one mediator between God and men, the man Christ Jesus. 1 Timothy 2:5

Patient Lord

God is patient, but we shouldn't let that make us think our sin is no big deal to him. He is patiently waiting for us to realize what a big deal it is—so big that my grandchildren and great grandchildren will be impacted by my bad choices. Tell God how much you appreciate his patience toward you as you struggle today to learn to live as his child.

> Then the LORD came down in the cloud and stood there with him and proclaimed his name, the LORD. And he passed in front of Moses, proclaiming,
>
> "The LORD, the LORD,
>   the compassionate and gracious God,
> slow to anger,
>   abounding in love and faithfulness,
> maintaining love to thousands,
>   and forgiving wickedness, rebellion and sin.
> Yet he does not leave the guilty unpunished;
>   he punishes the children and their children
> for the sin of the fathers
>   to the third and fourth generation." Exodus 34:5-8

> What if God, although choosing to show his wrath and make his power known, bore with great patience the objects of his wrath—prepared for destruction? What if he did this to make the riches of his glory known to the objects of his mercy, whom he prepared in advance for glory—even us, whom he also called, not only from the Jews but also from the Gentiles? Romans 9.22-24

Adoration

The Lord is not slow in keeping his promise, as some understand slowness. He is patient with you, not wanting anyone to perish, but everyone to come to repentance. 2 Peter 3:9

I was shown mercy so that in me, the worst of sinners, Christ Jesus might display his unlimited patience as an example for those who would believe on him and receive eternal life. 1 Timothy 1:16

[Fix] our eyes on Jesus, the pioneer and perfecter of faith. For the joy set before him he endured the cross, scorning its shame, and sat down at the right hand of the throne of God. Hebrews 12:2

The Ever-Present One

There is no place you can find yourself that God is not there. The Lord met Hagar, Sarah's Egyptian slave, alone and rejected in the desert. Praise God that no matter how bleak your problems appear, even if you wanted to, you couldn't get away from him.

> The eyes of the Lord are everywhere,
>   keeping watch on the wicked and the good.
>   Proverbs 15:3

> When you pray, go into your room, close the door and pray to your Father, who is unseen. Then your Father, who sees what is done in secret, will reward you. Matthew 6:6

> "Am I only a God nearby,"
>   declares the Lord,
> "and not a God far away?
> Who can hide in secret places
>   so that I cannot see them?"
>   declares the Lord.
> "Do not I fill heaven and earth?"
>   declares the Lord. Jeremiah 23:23-24

> But will God really dwell on earth? The heavens, even the highest heaven, cannot contain you. 1 Kings 8:27

> My Presence will go with you, and I will give you rest. Exodus 33:14b

> [Hagar] gave this name to the Lord who spoke to her: "You are the God who sees me,"

Adoration

for she said, "I have now seen the One who sees me." Genesis 16:13

Where can I go from your Spirit?
    Where can I flee from your presence?
If I go up to the heavens, you are there;
    if I make my bed in the depths, you are there.
If I rise on the wings of the dawn,
    if I settle on the far side of the sea,
even there your hand will guide me,
    your right hand will hold me fast.
If I say, "Surely the darkness will hide me
    and the light become night around me,"
even the darkness will not be dark to you;
    the night will shine like the day,
    for darkness is as light to you. Psalm 139:7-12

Our Refuge

God is the one to whom we can turn when the world seems to be caving in on us. He doesn't promise to take us out of the circumstances (the earth may still give way and the mountain fall), but he will not desert us. As you read, praise him for a specific time when you cried out to him and he heard you. That time may be right now.

> Trust in him at all times, you people;
> > pour out your hearts to him,
> > for God is our refuge. Psalm 62:8

> I call on you, my God, for you will answer me;
> > turn your ear to me and hear my prayer.
> Show the wonder of your great love,
> > you who save by your right hand
> > those who take refuge in you from their foes.
> > Psalm 17:6-7

> I love you, LORD, my strength.
> The LORD is my rock, my fortress and my deliverer;
> > my God is my rock, in whom I take refuge.
> He is my shield and the horn of my salvation,
> > my stronghold. Psalm 18:1-2

> God is our refuge and strength,
> > an ever-present help in trouble.
> Therefore we will not fear, though the earth give way
> > and the mountains fall into the heart of the sea,
> though its waters roar and foam
> > and the mountains quake with their surging.
> > Psalm 46:1-3

Adoration

Whoever dwells in the shelter of the Most High
    will rest in the shadow of the Almighty.
I will say of the Lord, "He is my refuge and my fortress,
    my God, in whom I trust."

Surely he will save you from the fowler's snare
    and from the deadly pestilence.
He will cover you with his feathers,
    and under his wings you will find refuge;
his faithfulness will be your shield and rampart.

You will not fear the terror of night,
    nor the arrow that flies by day,
nor the pestilence that stalks in the darkness,
    nor the plague that destroys at midday.

A thousand may fall at your side,
    ten thousand at your right hand,
    but it will not come near you. Psalm 91:1-7

The Lord has become my fortress,
    and my God the rock in whom I take refuge.
    Psalm 94:22

God of Revelation

God shows us his power and creativity in nature. He lets us know his character and standards in his Word. And he allowed us to see, hear and touch him, and know his love and friendship when he became a man. As you meditate, praise the God who makes himself known—in nature, the Bible and Jesus Christ.

> You will seek me and find me when you seek me with all your heart. I will be found by you," declares the Lord. Jeremiah 29:13-14a

The heavens declare the glory of God;
    the skies proclaim the work of his hands.
Day after day they pour forth speech;
    night after night they reveal knowledge.
They have no speech, they use no words;
    no sound is heard from them.
Yet their voice goes out into all the earth,
    their words to the ends of the world.
In the heavens God has pitched a tent for the sun…

The law of the Lord is perfect,
    refreshing the soul.
The statutes of the Lord are trustworthy,
    making wise the simple.
The precepts of the Lord are right,
    giving joy to the heart.
The commands of the Lord are radiant,
    giving light to the eyes.
The fear of the Lord is pure,
    enduring forever.
The ordinances of the Lord are firm

Adoration

and all of them are righteous.
They are more precious than gold,
　　than much pure gold;
they are sweeter than honey,
　　than honey from the honeycomb. Psalm 19:1-4, 7-10

In the past God spoke to our ancestors through the prophets at many times and in various ways, but in these last days he has spoken to us by his Son, whom he appointed heir of all things, and through whom he made the universe. Hebrews 1:1-2

My eyes have seen your salvation,
　　which you have prepared in the sight of all people,
a light for revelation to the Gentiles
　　and the glory of your people Israel. Luke 2:30-32

Anyone who has seen me has seen the Father... Believe me when I say that I am in the Father and the Father is in me. John 14:9b, 11a

The Lord, Our Righteousness

God's righteousness is often linked to justice as though righteousness does not tolerate injustice and oppression. It is his nature, and he is incapable of wrong. As you meditate on these verses, praise him because his moral law can be counted upon. It doesn't change from decade to decade. And he makes no mistakes when he judges the earth.

> This is the name by which he will be called:
>   The Lord Our Righteous Savior. Jeremiah 23:6b

> He is the Rock, his works are perfect,
>   and all his ways are just.
> A faithful God who does no wrong,
>   upright and just is he. Deuteronomy 32:4

> My salvation will last forever,
>   my righteousness will never fail. Isaiah 51:6c

> Lord, the God of Israel, you are righteous! We are left this day as a remnant. Here we are before you in our guilt, though because of it not one of us can stand in your presence. Ezra 9:15

> I will give thanks to the Lord
>   because of his righteousness;
> I will sing the praises of the name
>   of the Lord Most High. Psalm 7:17

> The Lord reigns forever;
>   he has established his throne for judgment.
> He will judge the world in righteousness;
>   he will govern the peoples with justice. Psalm 9:7-8

Adoration

For the Lord is righteous,
    he loves justice;
        upright men will see his face. Psalm 11:7

Clouds and thick darkness surround him;
    righteousness and justice are the foundation
of his throne. Psalm 97:2

Glorious and majestic are his deeds,
    and his righteousness endures forever. Psalm 111:3

You are righteous, Lord,
    and your laws are right.
The statutes you have laid down are righteous;
    they are fully trustworthy. Psalm 119:137-138

The Lord loves righteousness and justice;
    the earth is full of his unfailing love. Psalm 33:5

Your righteousness is like the highest mountains,
    your justice like the great deep. Psalm 36:6a

You answer us with awesome and righteous deeds,
    God our Savior
the hope of all the ends of the earth
    and of the farthest seas. Psalm 65:5

My mouth will tell of your righteous deeds,
    of your saving acts all day long—
    though I know not how to relate them...
Your righteousness, God, reaches to the heavens,
    you have done great things.
    Who is like you, God? Psalm 71:15, 19

Our Savior

God is not only our Refuge in trouble. He also saves us from our own sin, its power to control us and the consequences of an eternity separated from him. Praise him for bearing your burden and ask him to give you the power to say "No" to temptation.

> Praise be to the Lord, to God our Savior,
> > who daily bears our burdens.
>
> Our God is a God who saves;
> > from the Sovereign LORD
> > comes escape from death. Psalm 68:19-20

> The LORD your God is with you,
> > The Mighty Warrior who saves.
>
> He will take great delight in you;
> > in his love he will no longer rebuke you,
>
> but will rejoice over you with singing. Zephaniah 3:17

> "For God so loved the world that he gave his one and only Son, that whoever believes in him shall not perish but have eternal life. For God did not send his Son into the world to condemn the world, but to save the world through him. John 3:16-17

> For the grace of God has appeared that offers salvation to all people. It teaches us to say "No" to ungodliness and worldly passions, and to live self-controlled, upright and godly lives in this present age, while we wait for the blessed hope—the appearing of the glory of our great God and Savior, Jesus Christ, who gave himself for us to redeem us from all wickedness and to

Adoration

purify for himself a people that are his very own, eager to do what is good. Titus 2:11-14

Are not two sparrows sold for a penny? Yet not one of them will fall to the ground outside your Father's care. And even the very hairs of your head are all numbered. So don't be afraid; you are worth more than many sparrows. Matthew 10:29-31

I waited patiently for the LORD;
    he turned to me and heard my cry.

He lifted me out of the slimy pit,
    out of the mud and mire;
he set my feet on a rock
    and gave me a firm place to stand.

He put a new song in my mouth,
    a hymn of praise to our God.
Many will see and fear
    and put their trust in the LORD.

Blessed is the man
    who makes the LORD his trust,
who does not look to the proud,
    to those who turn aside to false gods. Psalm 40:1-4

To him who is able to keep you from stumbling and to present you before his glorious presence without fault and with great joy— to the only God our Savior be glory, majesty, power and authority, through Jesus Christ our Lord, before all ages, now and forevermore! Amen. Jude 24-25

The Good Shepherd

The picture of sheep grazing peacefully is God's ideal for our life with him. He cares for us as a shepherd protects his sheep, leading them to food and water and standing between them and danger. As you praise him, rest in his arms like a lamb and commit yourself to follow where your Shepherd leads.

> He brought his people out like a flock;
> > he led them like sheep through the wilderness.
> > Psalm 78:52

> He will stand and shepherd his flock
> > in the strength of the Lord,
> > in the majesty of the name of the LORD his God.
> And they will live securely,
> > for then his greatness
> > will reach to the ends of the earth. Micah 5:4

> He tends his flock like a shepherd:
> > He gathers the lambs in his arms
> and carries them close to his heart;
> > he gently leads those that have young. Isaiah 40:11

> The LORD is my shepherd,
> > I lack nothing.
> He makes me lie down in green pastures,
> > he leads me beside quiet waters,
> > he refreshes my soul.
> He guides me along the right paths
> > for his name's sake.
> Even though I walk through the darkest valley ,
> > I will fear no evil, for you are with me;

Adoration

your rod and your staff,
    they comfort me.
You prepare a table before me
    in the presence of my enemies.
You anoint my head with oil;
    my cup overflows.
Surely your goodness and love will follow me
    all the days of my life,
and I will dwell in the house of the LORD forever.
    Psalm 23

"I am the good shepherd. The good shepherd lays down his life for the sheep... I am the good shepherd; I know my sheep and my sheep know me—just as the Father knows me and I know the Father—and I lay down my life for the sheep. I have other sheep that are not of this sheep pen. I must bring them also. They too will listen to my voice, and there shall be one flock and one shepherd. John 10:11, 14-16

Now may the God of peace, who through the blood of the eternal covenant brought back from the dead our Lord Jesus, that great Shepherd of the sheep, equip you with everything good for doing his will, and may he work in us what is pleasing to him, through Jesus Christ, to whom be glory for ever and ever. Amen. Hebrews 13:20-21

For the Lamb at the center of the throne
    will be their shepherd;
he will lead them to springs of living water.
And God will wipe away every tear from their eyes.
    Revelation 7:17

The Sovereign Lord

The Sovereign reigns. His word is law. No president, dictator, or prime minister can make a decision without God's permission. Praise him because your own life is in his hands.

> Lord, God of our ancestors, are you not the God who is in heaven? You rule over all the kingdoms of the nations. Power and might are in your hand, and no one can withstand you. 2 Chronicles 20:6

> Nations are in uproar, kingdoms fall;
>   he lifts his voice, the earth melts.
> The Lord Almighty is with us;
>   the God of Jacob is our fortress.
> Come and see what the Lord has done,
>   the desolations he has brought on the earth.
> He makes wars cease to the ends of the earth;
>   he breaks the bow and shatters the spear,
>   he burns the shields with fire.
> He says, "Be still, and know that I am God;
>   I will be exalted among the nations,
>   I will be exalted in the earth." Psalm 46:6-10

> Our God is in heaven;
>   he does whatever pleases him. Psalm 115:3

> I know that you can do all things;
>   no purpose of yours can be thwarted. Job 42:2

> In the Lord's hand the king's heart is a stream of water
>   that he channels toward all who please him.
>   Proverbs 21:1

Adoration

Who can speak and have it happen
 if the Lord has not decreed it?
Is it not from the mouth of the Most High
 that both calamities and good things come?
Lamentations 3:37-38

All the trees of the forest will know that I the Lord bring down the tall tree and make the low tree grow tall. I dry up the green tree and make the dry tree flourish. I the Lord have spoken, and I will do it. Ezekiel 17:24

His dominion is an eternal dominion;
 his kingdom endures from generation to generation.
All the peoples of the earth are regarded as nothing.

He does as he pleases with the powers of heaven
 and the peoples of the earth.
No one can hold back his hand
 or say to him: "What have you done?" Daniel 4:34-35

In him we were also chosen, having been predestined according to the plan of him who works out everything in conformity with the purpose of his will, in order that we, who were the first to put our hope in Christ, might be for the praise of his glory. Ephesians 1:11-12

Spirit

God is not a man, but a spirit—unseen, but real. He has placed his spirit within us as the guarantee of his promise, enabling us to worship him in spirit and in truth. As you praise the Holy Spirit, open your heart to be filled with his freedom and power.

> In the beginning God created the heavens and the earth. Now the earth was formless and empty, darkness was over the surface of the deep, and the Spirit of God was hovering over the waters. Genesis 1:1-2

> Suddenly a sound like the blowing of a violent wind came from heaven and filled the whole house where [the disciples] were sitting. They saw what seemed to be tongues of fire that separated and came to rest on each of them. All of them were filled with the Holy Spirit and began to speak in other tongues as the Spirit enabled them. Acts 2:2-4

This is what was spoken by the prophet Joel:

> In the last days, God says,
>   I will pour out my Spirit on all people.
> Your sons and daughters will prophesy,
>   your young men will see visions,
>   your old men will dream dreams.
> Even on my servants, both men and women,
> I will pour out my Spirit in those days,
>   and they will prophesy. Acts 2:16-18

Adoration

[God] set his seal of ownership on us, and put his Spirit in our hearts as a deposit, guaranteeing what is to come. 2 Corinthians 1:22

And in him you too are being built together to become a dwelling in which God lives by his Spirit. Ephesians 2:22

The Spirit himself testifies with our spirit that we are God's children. Romans 8:16

The Spirit helps us in our weakness. We do not know what we ought to pray for, but the Spirit himself intercedes for us through wordless groans. And he who searches our hearts knows the mind of the Spirit, because the Spirit intercedes for God's people in accordance with the will of God. Romans 8: 26-27

The Spirit searches all things, even the deep things of God. For who knows a person's thoughts except their own spirit within them? In the same way no one knows the thoughts of God except the Spirit of God. What we have received is not the spirit of the world, but the Spirit who is from God, so that we may understand what God has freely given us. 1 Corinthian 2:10b-12

Now the Lord is the Spirit, and where the Spirit of the Lord is, there is freedom. And we, who with unveiled faces all reflect the Lord's glory, are being transformed into his image with ever-increasing glory, which comes from the Lord, who is the Spirit. 2 Corinthians 3:17-18

This is how you can recognize the Spirit of God: Every spirit that acknowledges that Jesus Christ has come in the flesh is from God, but every spirit that does not acknowledge Jesus is not from God. 1 John 4:2

God is spirit, and his worshipers must worship in the Spirit and in truth." John 4:24

The Suffering Servant

Although most people in Jesus' day, including his closest disciples, expected the Messiah to be a powerful king who would free them from Roman rule, the Old Testament prophet, Isaiah, described him very differently. Use this passage to meditate on what Christ did for you on the cross.

> Who has believed our message
> > and to whom has the arm of the Lord
> > > been revealed?
>
> He grew up before him like a tender shoot,
> > and like a root out of dry ground.
>
> He had no beauty or majesty to attract us to him,
> > nothing in his appearance
> > > that we should desire him.
>
> He was despised and rejected by mankind,
> > a man of sorrows, and familiar with suffering.
>
> Like one from whom people hide their faces
> > he was despised, and we esteemed him not.
>
> Surely he took up our pain
> > and bore our suffering,
>
> yet we considered him punished by God,
> > smitten by him, and afflicted.
>
> But he was pierced for our transgressions,
> > he was crushed for our iniquities;
>
> the punishment that brought us peace was on him,
> > and by his wounds we are healed.
>
> We all, like sheep, have gone astray,
> > each of us has turned to his own way;
>
> and the Lord has laid on him
> > the iniquity of us all.

He was oppressed and afflicted,
    yet he did not open his mouth;
he was led like a lamb to the slaughter,
    and as a sheep before her shearers is silent,
    so he did not open his mouth.
By oppression and judgment he was taken away.
    And who of his generation protested?
For he was cut off from the land of the living;
    for the transgression of my people
        he was punished.
He was assigned a grave with the wicked,
    and with the rich in his death,
though he had done no violence,
    nor was any deceit in his mouth.

Yet it was the LORD's will to crush him
    and cause him to suffer,
and though the LORD makes his life an offering for sin,
    he will see his offspring and prolong his days,
    and the will of the LORD will prosper in his hand.
After he has suffered,
    he will see the light of life and be satisfied;
by his knowledge my righteous servant will justify many,
    and he will bear their iniquities.
Therefore I will give him a portion among the great,
    and he will divide the spoils with the strong,
because he poured out his life unto death,
    and was numbered with the transgressors.
For he bore the sin of many,
    and made intercession for the transgressors.
    Isaiah 53

God of All Truth

There are things that are true for individuals: you like ice cream; I like brownies; you were born in Indiana; I was born in Minnesota. But God's truth is true for everyone and completely trustworthy. Praise God for the truth of his promises, and commit yourself to live in the light of his truth.

> Sovereign LORD, you are God! Your covenant is trustworthy, and you have promised these good things to your servant. 2 Samuel 7:28

> For the word of the Lord is right and true;
> he is faithful in all he does. Psalm 33:4

> Guide me in your truth and teach me,
> for you are God my Savior,
> and my hope is in you all day long. Psalm 25:5

> Jesus answered, "I am the way and the truth and the life. No one comes to the Father except through me. John 14:6

> All your words are true;
> all your righteous laws are eternal. Psalm 119:160

> The unfolding of your words gives light; Psalm 119:130a

> You, Lord, are my lamp;
> the LORD turns my darkness into light.
> 2 Samuel 22:29

> The light shines in the darkness, but the darkness has not overcome it.

There came a man sent from God whose name was John. He came as a witness to testify concerning that light, so that through him all might believe. He himself was not the light; he came only as a witness to the light. The true light that gives light to everyone was coming into the world. John 1:5-9

[Jesus] said, "I am the light of the world. Whoever follows me will never walk in darkness, but will have the light of life." John 8:12

"When the Advocate comes, whom I will send to you from the Father—the Spirit of truth who goes out from the Father—he will testify about me. John 15:26

But when he, the Spirit of truth, comes, he will guide you into all truth. He will not speak on his own; he will speak only what he hears, and he will tell you what is yet to come. He will glorify me because it is from me that he will receive what he will make known to you. John 16:13-15

The Unchanging One

God's character and his purpose to reconcile the world to himself do not change. The God who revealed himself in the Old Testament and became flesh in the New Testament is the same God who acts in my life and in the world of the twenty-first century. Praise him for his dependability.

> God said to Moses, "I AM WHO I AM. This is what you are to say to the Israelites: 'I AM has sent me to you.'" Exodus 3:14

> God is not human, that he should lie,
>   nor a human being,
>   that he should change his mind.
> Does he speak and then not act?
>   Does he promise and not fulfill? Numbers 23:19

> But the plans of the LORD stand firm forever,
>   the purposes of his heart through all generations.
>   Psalm 33:11

> In the beginning you laid the foundations of the earth,
>   and the heavens are the work of your hands.
> They will perish, but you remain;
>   they will all wear out like a garment.
> Like clothing you will change them
>   and they will be discarded.
> But you remain the same,
>   and your years will never end. Psalm 102:25-27

> "I the LORD do not change. So you, the descendants of Jacob, are not destroyed. Malachi 3:6

Because God wanted to make the unchanging nature of his purpose very clear to the heirs of what was promised, he confirmed it with an oath. God did this so that, by two unchangeable things in which it is impossible for God to lie, we who have fled to take hold of the hope set before us may be greatly encouraged. We have this hope as an anchor for the soul, firm and secure. Hebrews 6.17-19a

Every good and perfect gift is from above, coming down from the Father of the heavenly lights, who does not change like shifting shadows. James 1:17

Jesus Christ is the same yesterday and today and forever. Hebrews 13:8

The Way

Jesus described himself as both a road and a gate. As you meditate on these verses, praise the One who shows you the way to live and gives access to the Father.

Jesus answered, "I am the way and the truth and the life. No one comes to the Father except through me. John 14:6

I instruct you in the way of wisdom
   and lead you along straight paths.
When you walk, your steps will not be hampered;
   when you run, you will not stumble. Proverbs 4:11-12

Enter through the narrow gate. For wide is the gate and broad is the road that leads to destruction, and many enter through it. But small is the gate and narrow the road that leads to life, and only a few find it. Matthew 7:13-14

Whether you turn to the right or to the left, your ears will hear a voice behind you, saying, "This is the way; walk in it." Isaiah 30:21

And a highway will be there;
it will be called the Way of Holiness.
it will be for those who walk in that Way;
The unclean will not journey on it;
   wicked fools will not go about on it.

No lion will be there,
   nor any ravenous beast;

> they will not be found there.
> But only the redeemed will walk there,
> > and those the Lord has rescued will return.
> They will enter Zion with singing;
> > everlasting joy will crown their heads.
> Gladness and joy will overtake them,
> > and sorrow and sighing will flee away. Isaiah 35:8-10

> I will lead them beside streams of water
> on a level path where they will not stumble,
> because I am Israel's father,
> and Ephraim is my firstborn son. Jeremiah 31:9b

Therefore Jesus said again, "Very truly I tell you, I am the gate for the sheep. All who have come before me are thieves and robbers, but the sheep have not listened to them. I am the gate; whoever enters through me will be saved. They will come in and go out, and find pasture. John 10: 7-9

And when Jesus had cried out again in a loud voice, he gave up his spirit. At that moment the curtain of the temple was torn in two from top to bottom. The earth shook and the rocks split. Matthew 27: 50-51

Therefore, brothers and sisters, since we have confidence to enter the Most Holy Place by the blood of Jesus, by a new and living way opened for us through the curtain, that is, his body, and since we have a great priest over the house of God, let us draw near to God with a sincere heart and with the full assurance that faith brings, having our hearts sprinkled to cleanse us from a guilty conscience and having our bodies washed with pure water. Hebrews 10:19-22

Wise God

Sometimes God's wisdom seems foolish by human standards, for example, entering the world as a baby to forgive thieves, adulterers and murderers. But God's wisdom is based on his goodness and his complete knowledge. As you read, praise him for the ways in which you see his wisdom at work in your own life.

> But Joseph said to [his brothers] "Don't be afraid. Am I in the place of God? You intended to harm me, but God intended it for good to accomplish what is now being done, the saving of many lives. So then, don't be afraid. Genesis 50:19-21a

> "For my thoughts are not your thoughts,
>   neither are your ways my ways,"
>   declares the LORD.
> "As the heavens are higher than the earth,
>   so are my ways higher than your ways
>   and my thoughts than your thoughts. Isaiah 55:8-9

> Praise be to the name of God forever and ever;
>   wisdom and power are his.
> He changes times and seasons;
>   he deposes kings and raises up others.
> He gives wisdom to the wise
>   and knowledge to the discerning.
> He reveals deep and hidden things;
>   he knows what lies in darkness,
>   and light dwells with him. Daniel 2:20-22

> To God belong wisdom and power;
>   counsel and understanding are his. Job 12:13

Jesus said, "I praise you, Father, Lord of heaven and earth, because you have hidden these things from the wise and learned, and revealed them to little children. Yes, Father, for this was what you were pleased to do. Matthew 11:25-26

We preach Christ crucified: a stumbling block to Jews and foolishness to Gentiles, but to those whom God has called, both Jews and Greeks, Christ the power of God and the wisdom of God. For the foolishness of God is wiser than human wisdom, and the weakness of God is stronger than human strength. 1 Corinthians 1:23-25

But God chose the foolish things of the world to shame the wise; God chose the weak things of the world to shame the strong. God chose the lowly things of this world and the despised things—and the things that are not—to nullify the things that are, so that no one may boast before him. It is because of him that you are in Christ Jesus, who has become for us wisdom from God—that is, our righteousness, holiness and redemption. 1 Corinthians 1:27-30

Oh, the depth of the riches
   of the wisdom and knowledge of God!
How unsearchable his judgments,
   and his paths beyond tracing out!
Who has known the mind of the Lord?
   Or who has been his counselor?"
Who has ever given to God,
   that God should repay him?"
For from him and through him and to him are all things.
   To him be the glory forever! Amen. Romans 11:33-36

The Word made Flesh

Jesus didn't become God when he was born in Bethlehem or at some later time in his life. He is an eternal part of the Trinity, the eloquent expression of who God is and what he is like. Praise him because he lived among us and made it possible for you to become a child of God.

> In the beginning was the Word, and the Word was with God, and the Word was God. He was with God in the beginning.
>
> Through him all things were made; without him nothing was made that has been made. In him was life, and that life was the light of all mankind. The light shines in the darkness, but the darkness has not overcome it.
>
> There came a man sent from God whose name was John. He came as a witness to testify concerning that light, so that through him all might believe. He himself was not the light; he came only as a witness to the light.
>
> The true light that gives light to everyone was coming into the world. He was in the world, and though the world was made through him, the world did not recognize him. He came to that which was his own, but his own did not receive him. Yet to all who receive him, to those who believed in his name, he gave the right to become children of God— children born not of natural descent, nor of human decision or a husband's will, but born of God.

The Word became flesh and made his dwelling among us. We have seen his glory, the glory of the one and only Son, who came from the Father, full of grace and truth. John 1:1-14

I saw heaven standing open and there before me was a white horse, whose rider is called Faithful and True. With justice he judges and wages war. His eyes are like blazing fire, and on his head are many crowns. He has a name written on him that no one knows but he himself. He is dressed in a robe dipped in blood, and his name is the Word of God. Revelation 19:11-13

God of Wrath

God is patient, waiting for us to repent, but he hates sin, and he will punish evil. This should make us think twice about trying to run our own lives. It is also reason to rejoice because the child abuser who was never exposed, the employer who cheated his workers, and the dictator who imprisoned and killed his opposition will not get away with their sin. As you read, praise the God whose anger will not tolerate evil.

> Go, my people, enter your rooms
>   and shut the doors behind you;
> hide yourselves for a little while
>   until his wrath has passed by.
> See, the LORD is coming out of his dwelling
>   to punish the people of the earth for their sins.
> The earth will disclose the blood shed upon it;
>   she will conceal its slain no longer. Isaiah 26:20-21

> At your rebuke, God of Jacob,
>   both horse and chariot lie still.
> It is you alone who are to be feared.
>   Who can stand before you when you are angry?
> From heaven you pronounced judgment,
>   and the land feared and was quiet—
> when you, God, rose up to judge,
>   to save all the afflicted of the land.
> Surely your wrath against men brings you praise,
>   and the survivors of your wrath are restrained.
> Psalm 76:6-10

> I take no pleasure in the death of the wicked, but rather that they turn from their ways and live. Turn! Turn from your evil ways! Why will you die, people of Israel? Ezekiel 33:11b

Honey from the Comb

But the LORD is the true God;
    he is the living God, the eternal King.
When he is angry, the earth trembles;
    the nations cannot endure his wrath. Jeremiah 10:10

The LORD is slow to anger and great in power;
    the LORD will not leave the guilty unpunished.
His way is in the whirlwind and the storm,
    and clouds are the dust of his feet. Nahum 1:3

The wrath of God is being revealed from heaven against all the godlessness and wickedness of people, who suppress the truth by their wickedness. Romans 1:18

But the day of the Lord will come like a thief. The heavens will disappear with a roar; the elements will be destroyed by fire, and the earth and everything in it will be laid bare. 2 Peter 3:10

I saw heaven standing open and there before me was a white horse, whose rider is called Faithful and True. With justice he judges and wages war. His eyes are like blazing fire, and on his head are many crowns. He has a name written on him that no one knows but he himself. He is dressed in a robe dipped in blood, and his name is the Word of God. The armies of heaven were following him, riding on white horses and dressed in fine linen, white and clean. Coming out of his mouth is a sharp sword with which to strike down the nations. "He will rule them with an iron scepter." He treads the winepress of the fury of the wrath of God Almighty. On his robe and on his thigh he has this name written:

    KING OF KINGS AND LORD OF LORDS. Revelation 19:11-16

Part II:
Confession

Confession

> Search me, O God, and know my heart;
>   test me and know my anxious thoughts.
> See if there is any offensive way in me,
>   and lead me in the way everlasting. Psalm 139:23-24

When we have really thought about what God is like, we realize that we aren't as good as we would like people to think we are. Isaiah was a young prophet when he had a vision of God in the temple (Isaiah 6). His response wasn't "Wow! What a great worship experience!" It was "Oh, no! I'm ruined! I have such a dirty mouth, and everyone around me has a dirty mouth!" He was embarrassed when he compared himself to God instead of to other people.

Confession is telling God that he is right about our sin, saying we are sorry and asking him to forgive us. Chances are you won't have any trouble thinking of something fresh that embarrasses you when you compare yourself to the God you have been adoring, but these verses with their questions are intended to help you examine your life. If you love God, you will want to be rid of all that displeases him. Tell him you are sorry and get on with it. He has promised to forgive.

> If we confess our sins, he is faithful and just and will forgive us our sins and purify us from all unrighteousness. 1 John 1:9

Daily Confession

Some things we do we don't even realize are wrong. Ask God to show you, so you can stop.

Other things we do we know very well are wrong, bad habits that can easily get control of our lives. That's what the psalm writer means by "willful sins." Ask God to give you the strength to resist them.

The sins that we do on the outside all start inside our minds, so ask God to keep the things you say and think about pleasing to him.

Who can discern his errors?
    Forgive my hidden faults.

Keep your servant also from willful sins;
    may they not rule over me.

Then will I be blameless,
    innocent of great transgression.

May the words of my mouth
    and the meditations of my heart
    be pleasing in your sight,

O Lord, my Rock and my Redeemer. Psalm 19:13-14

Ten Commandments
Exodus 20:3-17

The first four commandments given to Moses on Mount Sinai set the standard for loving the Lord our God with all our heart, soul, mind and strength. The last six give a few of the specifics that Jesus summarized as loving our neighbor as ourselves. Use the questions following each commandment to examine your own life.

I. You shall have no other gods before me.
   Is God the most important thing in my life?

II. You shall not make for yourself an image in the form of anything in heaven above or on the earth beneath or in the waters below.
   Is there anything I put ahead of God and make into an idol—sports, success, family, health or even my church?

III. You shall not misuse the name of the LORD your God, for the LORD will not hold anyone guiltless who misuses his name.
   Do I call Jesus 'Lord' but fail to obey him? Do I say God's name lightly when I'm not really thinking about who he is or what he has done for me?

IV. Remember the Sabbath day by keeping it holy. Six days you shall labor and do all your work, but the seventh day is a Sabbath to the LORD your God.
   Do I treat Sunday as my day or the Lord's Day? How is my balance of rest and worship on that day?

V. Honor your father and your mother, so that you may live long in the land the LORD your God is giving you.
> How do I show respect for my parents?

VI. You shall not murder
> Jesus said hate and disrespect are as bad as murder.

VII. You shall not commit adultery.
> Jesus said thinking about having sex with someone is the same as doing it.

VIII. You shall not steal.
> Do I take anything that does not belong to me? Small things left unattended? My employer's time? Unfair advantage?

IX. You shall not give false testimony against your neighbor.
> Is all that I say honest and kind? Does my talk hurt my neighbor's reputation?

X. You shall not covet your neighbor's house. You shall not covet your neighbor's wife, or his male or female servant, his ox or donkey, or anything that belongs to your neighbor.
> Am I content with what God has given me, or am I greedy for all I see in advertisements?

A Higher Law
Matthew 5:21-45, 48

Jesus said he had not come to destroy the law, but to fulfill it (Matthew 15:17). In fact, in his Sermon on the Mount he raised the standard from mere outward conformity to inner godliness. As you read these verses, talk to God about the ways in which you have failed to meet his standards.

> You have heard that it was said to the people long ago, 'You shall not murder, and anyone who murders will be subject to judgment.' But I tell you that anyone who is angry with a brother or sister, will be subject to judgment. Again, anyone who says to a brother or sister, 'Raca,' is answerable to the court. And anyone who says, 'You fool!' will be in danger of the fire of hell.

> Am I holding on to anger or resentment against those who may have wronged me? Do I look down on or insult those who are different from me?

> You have heard that it was said, 'You shall not commit adultery.' But I tell you that anyone who looks at a woman lustfully has already committed adultery with her in his heart

> Am I keeping my mind and body pure for my life partner whether or not I have met him or her yet?

> It has been said, 'Anyone who divorces his wife must give her a certificate of divorce.' But I tell you that anyone who divorces his wife, except for sexual immorality, makes her the victim of adultery, and

anyone who marries a divorced woman commits adultery.

> Am I committed to faithfully keeping my vows even when the marriage doesn't turn out like I had dreamed?

Again, you have heard that it was said to the people long ago, 'Do not break your oath, but fulfill to the Lord the vows you have made.' But I tell you, do not swear an oath at all... All you need to say is simply 'Yes' or 'No'; anything beyond this comes from the evil one.

> Am I so honest that no one who knows me would ever question the integrity of what I say?

You have heard that it was said, 'Eye for eye, and tooth for tooth.' But I tell you, do not resist an evil person. If anyone slaps you on the right cheek, turn to them the other cheek also. And if anyone wants to sue you and take your shirt, hand over your coat as well. If anyone forces you to go one mile, go with them two miles. Give to the one who asks you, and do not turn away from the one who wants to borrow from you

> When someone wrongs me or makes demands on me, do I resist or try to get even, or do I do something good for him as Christ would?

You have heard that it was said, 'Love your neighbor and hate your enemy.' But I tell you, love your enemies and pray for those who persecute you, that you may be children of your Father in heaven.

> Do I pray for those who dislike me or my country and look for ways to befriend them?

<blockquote>
Be perfect, therefore,
as your heavenly Father is perfect
</blockquote>

Beatitudes

Matthew 5:3-10

Jesus began the Sermon on the Mount by redefining what he expected of the citizens of his kingdom. Examine your life to see how you measure up.[1]

Blessed are the poor in spirit, for theirs is the kingdom of heaven.
>Do I recognize my spiritual poverty—that nothing I can do will buy my way to heaven?

Blessed are those who mourn, for they will be comforted.
>Am I as unhappy about my sin as I would be if someone I loved died?

Blessed are the meek, for they will inherit the earth.
>Do I accept what God says is true of me, or do I try to act like I am more important than others around me?

Blessed are those who hunger and thirst for righteousness, for they will be filled.
>Do I go after what is right like a starving person craves food or a thirsty child cries for a drink?

Blessed are the merciful, for they will be shown mercy.
>Do I treat others with the same mercy I want from God?

---

[1] These questions are based on John R. W. Stott's *The Message of the Sermon on the Mount.*

Confession

Blessed are the pure in heart, for they will see God.
Do I have one untainted purpose—to serve God—or is my heart divided between conflicting goals and ambitions?

Blessed are the peacemakers, for they will be called children of God.
Have I done all I can to resolve quarrels in my family, community and internationally, or is there more my Lord wants me to do?

Blessed are those who are persecuted because of righteousness, for theirs is the kingdom of heaven.
Have I ever gone after what is right so hard that I rattled cages and drew criticism?

Such Were Some of You
1 Corinthians 6:9-11

Some of these sins may well have been part of our lives before we met Christ, but this baggage is not something we can take into heaven with us.

The first list below is sexual sins. Idolatry is included because in ancient times sexual acts were often a part of worshipping false gods. In our society the worship of physical beauty (sex appeal) is a serious problem. The second list has to do with 'stuff'—wanting more and being willing to do anything to get it.

Read the lists slowly as you think about what kind of hold these sins might still have on your life. Ask God to continue to remake you as a citizen of his kingdom.

> Do you not know that wrong doers will not inherit the kingdom of God?
>
> Do not be deceived:
>   Neither the sexually immoral
>   nor idolaters
>   nor adulterers
>   nor men who have sex with men
>
>   nor thieves
>   nor the greedy
>   nor drunkards
>   nor slanderers
>   nor swindlers
>   will inherit the kingdom of God.
>
> And that is what some of you were.
>   But you were washed,

> you were sanctified,
>   you were justified
> in the name of the Lord Jesus Christ
>   and by the Spirit of our God.

My Thoughts and Attitudes
Colossians 3:1, 5, 8-10

Jesus said it is not what goes into people as food that makes them unclean, but what comes out that reveals the state of their hearts (Matthew 15:11). Use these verses and questions to examine the thoughts and attitudes that matter so much to him.

> Since, then, you have been raised with Christ, set your hearts on things above, where Christ is, seated at the right hand of God...
>
>> Am I more concerned about what God is doing in my life and in the world or about my personal agenda?
>
> Put to death, therefore, whatever belongs to your earthly nature:
>
>> Do I hate my sin enough to not just lock it up where I could come back to it if I chose but to give it a lethal injection?
>
> sexual immorality,
>
>> Do I participate in sexual activities God has forbidden?
>
> impurity,
>
>> Have I let bits of the culture around me mix with the Kingdom culture to which God has called me?
>
> lust,
>
>> Do I allow myself to think about what God has forbidden, pretending it doesn't matter since I didn't actually do it?

Confession

evil desires
> Do I want anything that is going to make me uncomfortable in God's presence like Adam and Eve in the garden of Eden (Genesis 3)?

and greed, which is idolatry…
> Do I want more and more of the good things God has given, treating 'stuff' as if it were God?

But now you must also rid yourselves of all such things as these:

anger,
> When did I get angry this week?

rage,
> When I got angry, did I lose control?

malice,
> Do I harbor ill will against any individual or group, longing to see them suffer and delighting in their failures?

slander,
> Do I make hurtful comments about people I don't like?

and filthy language from your lips.
> Do I join in the gutter talk I hear around me?

Do not lie to each other, since you have taken off your old self with its practices and have put on the new self, which is being renewed in knowledge in the image of its Creator.

Am I just pretending to be a good Christian, lying to myself and my Christian friends, without letting Jesus replace my old self with a new identity in him?

More about My Thought Life
Philippians 4:4-8

As the Holy Spirit roots out the negative thoughts and attitudes, he wants to fill us with positive thoughts and attitudes. Use these verses to think more about your thought life.

Rejoice in the Lord always. I will say it again: Rejoice!
> Do I focus on the joy I have in Christ all the time, or just when circumstances make it easy to rejoice?

Let your gentleness be evident to all. The Lord is near.
> Does an aggressive personality get in the way of people seeing Jesus in me?

Do not be anxious about anything,
> What have I been worrying about lately instead of taking it to God?

but in every situation, by prayer and petition, with thanksgiving, present your requests to God.
> Do I pray with such faith that I can thank God ahead of time for his answers?

And the peace of God, which transcends all understanding, will guard your hearts and your minds in Christ Jesus.
> Where are my emotions and thinking vulnerable right now and in danger of missing God's peace?

Finally, brothers, whatever is true, whatever is noble, whatever is right, whatever is pure, whatever is lovely, whatever is admirable—if anything is excellent or praiseworthy—think about such things.

Where have I been wasting my time with lazy thinking about mediocre things that won't help me to be more like Jesus Christ and might even drag me down in Satan's lies?

Acts of the Sinful Nature
Galatians 5:19-21

Our culture tells us that these so-called 'sins' are perfectly normal. But they aren't 'normal' in one who has been made over by Jesus Christ and given his nature.

The acts of the sinful nature are obvious:

sexual immorality
    Do I let my passions control my sex life rather than my commitment to obey God?

impurity and debauchery;
    Have I let my testimony for Christ be diluted with an inappropriate lifestyle?

idolatry and witchcraft;
    Have I experimented with 'alternative spritualties' to get what I want, opening myself up to false gods and evil spirits?

hatred,
    Have I let resentments fester into hate?

discord,
    Am I critical and hard to get along with?

jealousy
    Do I resent those who have it better than me, rather than trusting God to supply my needs?

fits of rage,
    Do I let my temper get out of control?

selfish ambition,
> Am I so eager to succeed that I don't notice how I am hurting others?

dissensions,
> What is my attitude toward those in authority at work, at home, at church, and in the community?

factions and envy;
> Am I cliquish, going off with my own little group and muttering about others?

drunkenness,
> Do I use substances that tear down my God-given inhibitions and impair my judgment?

orgies, and the like.
> Do some of the parties and clubs I go to get out of hand?

I warn you, as I did before, that those who live like this will not inherit the kingdom of God.
> Am I willing to change my lifestyle if that's what it takes to be part of God's kingdom?

How I Treat Others
Psalm 15

What does a blameless life look like? As you pray, examine your attitudes and the way you treat other people.

> Lord, who may dwell in your sacred tent?
>   Who may live on your holy mountain?

> The one whose walk is blameless,
>> Could an enemy find something to blame me for in the way I live?

> who does what is righteous,
>> When have I failed to do the right thing?

> who speaks the truth from their heart;
>> When have I said something I didn't mean?

> whose tongue utters no slander,
>> What have I said that unfairly criticizes another?

> who does no wrong to a neighbor,
>> How have my words or actions hurt those around me?

> and casts no slur on others;
>> How have I implied disrespect for another person or group?

> who despises a vile person
>> Have I looked at sin as God does or have I joined the crowd in praising celebrities and powerful people who have no regard for God's law?

but honors those who fear the LORD;
>Do I openly show my respect for those whose lives are committed to God or do I laugh at how out of step they are?

who keeps an oath even when it hurts, and does not change their mind;
>Do I keep a promise even when it is to my disadvantage, or do I make excuses to get out of it?

who lends money to the poor without interest;
>Do I help those in need without thinking about what I will get out of it?

who does not accept a bribe against the innocent.
>Do I do what is right even if it means missing out on financial advantage?

Whoever does these things will never be shaken.

Love in Action

Romans 12:9-17

We all know that God wants us to love one another, but what does sincere love look like? In his letter to the church at Rome, the Apostle Paul spells out some specifics.

Love must be sincere.
   Do I really love others or have I merely learned to hide my true feelings behind a polite smile?

Hate what is evil; cling to what is good.
   If my love is sincere, what evils will I hate? What good will I cling to?

Be devoted to one another in love. Honor one another above yourselves.
   Am I devoted to others, or do I prefer honor for myself?

Never be lacking in zeal, but keep your spiritual fervor, serving the Lord.
   When did my zeal for serving the Lord flag this week?

Be joyful in hope,
   Could my lack of joy (and zeal) come from losing sight of the hope the Lord has set before me?

patient in affliction,
   When have I grown impatient with all the things going wrong in my life and perhaps taken it out on those around me?

faithful in prayer.
> How can I make prayer a higher priority in the midst of all that is going on?

Share with the Lord's people who are in need.
> How can I better show sincere love to Christians in need by my prayers, practical help or listening ear?

Practice hospitality.
> How might God want to use my home to show sincere love?

Bless those who persecute you; bless and do not curse.
> How sincere is my love for those who make my life difficult? Do I wish good or evil on them?

Rejoice with those who rejoice; mourn with those who mourn.
> Am I able to set aside my own emotions and share those of the people God has called me to love?

Live in harmony with one another.
> How could sincere love on my part heal the disharmony around me?

Do not be proud, but be willing to associate with people of low position.
> When has my pride kept me from associating with—and loving—someone God has put in my life?

Do not be conceited.
> How does my view of myself need to change in order for me to love sincerely?

Do not repay anyone evil for evil.
>   When did I last let my desire to get even overcome my commitment to sincere love?

Be careful to do what is right in the eyes of everyone.
>   Do I love others enough to make it a point to do what they consider "the right thing"?

Renewing Relationships
Ephesians 4:25-32

Healthy relationships require honesty, thoughtfulness, and consideration of others. Anger, malice and unwholesome talk are especially destructive. As you pray through these verses, ask God to show you where your relationships need his healing.

> Therefore each of you must put off falsehood and speak truthfully to your neighbor, for we are all members of one body.

In what areas of my life have I been putting up a false front that needs to come down for me to function as one body with other Christians?

> "In your anger do not sin": Do not let the sun go down while you are still angry, and do not give the devil a foothold.

Have I let anger and resentments give Satan a foothold in my life?

> Anyone who has been stealing must steal no longer, but must work, doing something useful with their own hands, that they may have something to share with those in need.

How have I been taking from others instead of working for their good?

> Do not let any unwholesome talk come out of your mouths, but only what is helpful for building others up according to their needs, that it may benefit those who listen.

> Does what I say or post on social media build others up or does it make it more difficult for them to grow in their relationship to Christ?

And do not grieve the Holy Spirit of God, with whom you were sealed for the day of redemption.
> What in my life makes the Holy Spirit sad?

Get rid of all bitterness, rage and anger, brawling and slander, along with every form of malice.
> Which of these do I need to get rid of for healthier relationships?

Be kind and compassionate to one another, forgiving each other, just as in Christ God forgave you.
> What can I do today to treat others more like God has treated me?

Avoiding the Suggestion of Evil
Ephesians 5:1-7

It's not enough to avoid committing actual sins. God wants my life to be so characterized by his love that there is not even a hint that I might be involved in sin. Use these verses to look at the impression you may be making on other people.

Follow God's example, therefore, as dearly loved children
> Do I long to be like my heavenly Father as much as children want to imitate their daddy?

and walk in the way of love, just as Christ loved us and gave himself up for us as a fragrant offering and sacrifice to God.
> Can others 'smell' God's love in me like a fragrant perfume?

But among you there must not be even a hint of sexual immorality,
> Does the way I dress and talk or the music I listen to suggest an acceptance of sexual immorality even if I'm not actually doing it?

or of any kind of impurity,
> Am I obviously sold out to God, or are there suggestions of competing allegiances in my words and actions?

or of greed, because these are improper for God's holy people.
> What clues would a look in my closet or at my credit card statement give to my values and priorities?

Nor should there be obscenity,
>Is my conversation in the locker room as clean as it would be at Bible study?

foolish talk
>Do I pass on gossip and rumors that don't build up others or Christ?

or coarse joking, which are out of place,
>Would Jesus find my jokes funny?

but rather thanksgiving.
>Is my conversation full of complaining or of appreciation for what God has done?

For of this you can be sure: No immoral, impure or greedy person—such a person is an idolater—has any inheritance in the kingdom of Christ and of God.
>Am I living as though physical and material pleasure were a more valuable inheritance than God's kingdom?

Let no one deceive you with empty words, for because of such things God's wrath comes on those who are disobedient. Therefore do not be partners with them.
>Have I fallen for the worldview of the mass media and popular culture and gone along with the crowd as a partner?

Prayer of National Confession
Daniel 9:4-11, 17-19

No modern political nation is God's kingdom on earth. Every culture has been tainted with sin. Both Daniel (in these verses) and Nehemiah (Nehemiah 1:5-11) model confession of the nation's sins as they seek revival in the land and the restoration of righteousness and justice. Pray Daniel's prayer, and at the ellipsis (...) insert some of the sins of our land that have troubled you such as those suggested. In the space at the end, add things you see in our nation that you know displease God.

Lord, the great and awesome God, who keeps his covenant of love with those who love him and keep his commandments, we have sinned and done wrong. We have been wicked and have rebelled; we have turned away from your commands and laws. We have not listened to your servants the prophets, who spoke in your name to our kings, our princes and our ancestors, and to all the people of the land.

Lord, you are righteous, but this day we are covered with shame... We and our kings, our princes and our ancestors are covered with shame, Lord, because we have sinned against you. The Lord our God is merciful and forgiving, even though we have rebelled against him; we have not obeyed the Lord our God or kept the laws he gave us through his servants the prophets. [We have] transgressed your law and turned away, refusing to obey you...

Confession

We have aborted our babies and abused our children.

We have substituted material things for quality relationships in our families.

We have demeaned marriage and broken our solemn vows.

We have filled our minds with violence from television, movies, and video games.

We have worshipped our bodies and physical beauty.

We have glorified celebrity instead of character.

We selfishly believe we deserve to satisfy our every whim with the result of rampant obesity and credit card debt.

We make snap judgements about our neighbors based on the way they dress, the color of their skin, or the language they speak at home, and assume that difference makes them somehow less deserving of our respect and concern.

We are so wrapped up in our own point of view that we ignore the concerns of those who see things differently and keep silent in the face of their suffering.

We have based our international policies on what brings us the greatest financial profit rather than on freedom and justice for all.

We have exploited the resources that you provided and disregarded the impact of our actions on the rest of your creation.

We are obsessed with our personal rights while remaining unconcerned about the good of our communities.

We trust in our own plans for security instead of in you, the Almighty God.

...Now, our God, hear the prayers and petitions of your servant. For your sake, Lord, look with favor on your desolate sanctuary. Give ear, our God, and hear; open your eyes and see the desolation of the city that bears your Name. We do not make requests of you because we are righteous, but because of your great mercy.

Lord, listen!
Lord, forgive!
Lord, hear and act!

For your sake, my God, do not delay, because your city and your people bear your Name.

Prayer of David
Psalm 51

Although King David is described as a man after God's own heart (1 Samuel 13:14), he used his position of power to seduce the wife of one of his most loyal soldiers. When he feared the scandal of her pregnancy, the king had her husband killed in a desperate cover up (2 Samuel 11-12). But David repented and turned from his sin.

No matter what you have done, you can humble yourself as David did in this psalm, and ask the God of grace to cleanse you and restore you to a full and joyful relationship with him.

> Have mercy on me, O God,
>   according to your unfailing love;
> according to your great compassion
>   blot out my transgressions.
> Wash away all my iniquity
>   and cleanse me from my sin.
> For I know my transgressions,
>   and my sin is always before me.
>
> Against you, you only, have I sinned
>   and done what is evil in your sight;
> so you are right in your verdict
>   and justified when you judge.
> Surely I was sinful at birth,
>   sinful from the time my mother conceived me.
> Yet you desired faithfulness even in the womb;
>   you taught me wisdom in that secret place.
>
> Cleanse me with hyssop, and I will be clean;
>   wash me, and I will be whiter than snow.

Honey from the Comb

Let me hear joy and gladness;
    let the bones you have crushed rejoice.
Hide your face from my sins
    and blot out all my iniquity.
Create in me a pure heart, O God,
    and renew a steadfast spirit within me.

Do not cast me from your presence
    or take your Holy Spirit from me.
Restore to me the joy of your salvation
    and grant me a willing spirit, to sustain me.
Then I will teach transgressors your ways,
    so that sinners will turn back to you.
Deliver me from the guilt of bloodshed, O God,
    you who are God my Savior,
    and my tongue will sing of your righteousness.
Open my lips, Lord,
    and my mouth will declare your praise.

You do not delight in sacrifice, or I would bring it;
    you do not take pleasure in burnt offerings.
My sacrifice, O God, is a broken spirit;
    a broken and contrite heart
    you, God, will not despise.
May it please you to prosper Zion,
    to build up the walls of Jerusalem.
Then you will delight in the sacrifices of the righteous,
    in burnt offerings offered whole;
    then bulls will be offered on your altar.

Part III:
Thanksgiving

Thanksgiving

Because of the Lord's great love we are not consumed,
  for his compassions never fail.
They are new every morning;
  great is your faithfulness. Lamentations 3:22-23

These verses by the prophet Jeremiah, written at a time of great national tragedy, remind us that the Lord's compassions are not just something that happened in Bible history or even in your own past, but are renewed daily. To keep thanksgiving fresh and specific, thank God for something he has done for you in the last twenty-four hours.

It may be
  an answer to prayer,
    a person he has brought into your life,
      an event where you see his hand, or
        a gift he has given you.

You may want to use a notebook or a bound journal to keep a "Blessing Book." Writing down and reviewing your list from time to time will keep you mindful of how good God has been to you.

The verses under Gratitude in the Supplication section of this book will remind you that a heart of thanksgiving is one of the things God desires from his people. Use the following passages to stimulate your prayers.

For Your Salvation
1 Timothy 1:12-18

The Apostle Paul came to Christ after years of believing he could be good enough for heaven if he kept a list of rules. He even chased down and imprisoned those who claimed salvation was a free gift from God. Yet God used this changed man to reach the world with the good news of salvation. As you read Paul's testimony, consider what Christ has saved you out of and give him thanks for using you.

> I thank Christ Jesus our Lord,
>   who has given me strength,
>   that he considered me trustworthy,
>   appointing me to his service.
>
> Even though I was once a blasphemer
>   and a persecutor
>   and a violent man,
>   I was shown mercy
>   because I acted in ignorance and unbelief.
>
> The grace of our Lord was poured out on me abundantly,
>   along with the faith
>   and love
>   that are in Christ Jesus.
>
> Here is a trustworthy saying that deserves full acceptance:
>
> Christ Jesus came into the world to save sinners—of whom I am the worst. But for that very reason I was shown mercy so that in me, the worst of sinners, Christ Jesus might display his immense patience as an example for those who would believe in him and receive eternal life.

For Spiritual Blessings
Ephesians 1:3-10

In his letter to the Ephesians, the Apostle Paul reminds them of a whole list of blessings we have received in Christ for which we should be thankful.

> Praise be to the God and Father of our Lord Jesus Christ, who has blessed us in the heavenly realms with every spiritual blessing in Christ.
>
> For he chose us in him before the creation of the world to be holy and blameless in his sight.
>
> In love he predestined us for adoption to sonship through Jesus Christ, in accordance with his pleasure and will
>
> —to the praise of his glorious grace, which he has freely given us in the One he loves.
>
> In him we have redemption through his blood,
>
> the forgiveness of sins,
>
> in accordance with the riches of God's grace that he lavished on us.
>
> With all wisdom and understanding, he made known to us the mystery of his will according to his good pleasure, which he purposed in Christ, to be put into effect when the times will have reached their fulfillment
>
> —to bring unity to all things in heaven and on earth under Christ.

For His Care

Psalm 23

Let this analogy of a shepherd caring for his sheep remind you of ways in which God has provided for you, disciplined you and protected you. Thank him for his presence in times of sorrow, suffering or opposition, and his promise to prepare a future home for you.

> The LORD is my shepherd, I lack nothing.
>
> He makes me lie down in green pastures,
> > he leads me beside quiet waters,
> > he refreshes my soul.
>
> He guides me along the right paths
> > for his name's sake.
>
> Even though I walk
> > through the darkest valley,
> I will fear no evil,
> > for you are with me;
> your rod and your staff,
> > they comfort me.
>
> You prepare a table before me
> > in the presence of my enemies.
> You anoint my head with oil;
> > my cup overflows.
>
> Surely your goodness and love will follow me
> > all the days of my life,
> and I will dwell in the house of the LORD
> > forever.

For Fellow Believers

The Apostle Paul thanked God for what he saw God doing in the churches to whom he addressed his letters. What have you seen in members of your church or other Christians you have known or heard about for which you should thank God?

> For this reason, ever since I heard about your faith in the Lord Jesus and your love for all God's people, I have not stopped giving thanks for you, remembering you in my prayers. Ephesians 1:15-16

> I always thank my God for you because of his grace given you in Christ Jesus. For in him you have been enriched in every way—with all kinds of speech and with all knowledge—God thus confirming our testimony about Christ among you. Therefore you do not lack any spiritual gift as you eagerly wait for our Lord Jesus Christ to be revealed. He will also keep you firm to the end, so that you will be blameless on the day of our Lord Jesus Christ. God is faithful, who has called you into fellowship with his Son, Jesus Christ our Lord. 1 Corinthians 1:4-11

> I thank my God every time I remember you. In all my prayers for all of you, I always pray with joy because of your partnership in the gospel from the first day until now, being confident of this, that he who began a good work in you will carry it on to completion until the day of Christ Jesus. Philippians 1:3-6

And we also thank God continually because, when you received the word of God, which you heard from us, you accepted it not as a human word, but as it actually is, the word of God, which is indeed at work in you who believe. 1 Thessalonians 2:13

We always thank God for all of you and continually mention you in our prayers. We remember before our God and Father your work produced by faith, your labor prompted by love, and your endurance inspired by hope in our Lord Jesus Christ. 1 Thessalonians 1:2-3

I thank my God through Jesus Christ for all of you, because your faith is being reported all over the world. Romans 1:8

We always thank God, the Father of our Lord Jesus Christ, when we pray for you, because we have heard of your faith in Christ Jesus and of the love you have for all God's people—the faith and love that spring from the hope stored up for you in heaven… Colossians 1:3-5a

Thanks be to God, who always leads us as captives in Christ's triumphal procession and uses us to spread the aroma of the knowledge of him everywhere. 2 Corinthians 2:14

For What God is Doing in the World
Jeremiah 32:17-19

As you pray the words of the prophet Jeremiah, think of specific situations you have read about in the news or with which you have personal contact that reveal God's greatness in creation, his love and mercy to his people or his judgment as he works out his plan of salvation in the world, and thank him for what he is accomplishing.

> Ah, Sovereign LORD, you have made the heavens and the earth by your great power and outstretched arm. Nothing is too hard for you.
>
> You show love to thousands but bring the punishment for the parents' sins into the laps of their children after them.
>
> O great and mighty God, whose name is the LORD Almighty, great are your purposes and mighty are your deeds.
>
> Your eyes are open to the ways of all mankind; you reward everyone according to their conduct and as their deeds deserve.
>
> You performed signs and wonders in Egypt and have continued them to this day, in Israel and among all mankind, and have gained the renown that is still yours.

For Answered Prayer
Psalm 66

The Israelites thanked God for bringing them out of Egypt and through the Red Sea. In these verses the psalmist remembers difficult times when God tested this people and brought them through. Thank God for some specific times in your life when he heard your cry for help and answered your prayers.

> Shout with joy to God, all the earth!
>   Sing the glory of his name;
>   make his praise glorious!
> Say to God, "How awesome are your deeds!
>   So great is your power
>   that your enemies cringe before you.
> All the earth bows down to you;
>   they sing praise to you,
>   they sing praise to your name."
>
> Come and see what God has done,
>   how awesome his works in man's behalf!
> He turned the sea into dry land,
>   they passed through the waters on foot—
>   come, let us rejoice in him.
> He rules forever by his power,
>   his eyes watch the nations—
>   let not the rebellious rise up against him.
>
> Praise our God, all peoples,
>   let the sound of his praise be heard;
> he has preserved our lives
>   and kept our feet from slipping.

Thanksgiving

For you, God, tested us;
    you refined us like silver.
You brought us into prison
    and laid burdens on our backs.
You let men ride over our heads;
    we went through fire and water,
    but you brought us to a place of abundance.

I will come to your temple with burnt offerings
    and fulfill my vows to you—
vows my lips promised and my mouth spoke
    when I was in trouble.
I will sacrifice fat animals to you
    and an offering of rams;
    I will offer bulls and goats.

Come and hear, all you who fear God;
    let me tell you what he has done for me.
I cried out to him with my mouth;
    his praise was on my tongue.

If I had cherished sin in my heart,
    the Lord would not have listened;
but God has surely listened
    and heard my voice in prayer.

Praise be to God,
    who has not rejected my prayer
    or withheld his love from me!

For Wealth and Honor

Rather than take credit for his own achievements, Israel's great King David acknowledged that his wealth and honor came from God. After him, the prophet Daniel acknowledged that his success in government service was not his own doing. As you read the words of these two men, consider the possessions and recognition that have been yours, and acknowledge God's role in those achievements.

> Praise be to you, LORD,
> > the God of our father Israel,
> > from everlasting to everlasting.
>
> Yours, LORD, is the greatness and the power
> > and the glory and the majesty and the splendor,
> > for everything in heaven and earth is yours.
>
> Yours, LORD, is the kingdom;
> > you are exalted as head over all.
>
> Wealth and honor come from you;
> > you are the ruler of all things.
>
> In your hands are strength and power
> > to exalt and give strength to all.
>
> Now, our God, we give you thanks,
> > and praise your glorious name.
>
> But who am I, and who are my people, that we should be able to give as generously as this? Everything comes from you, and we have given you only what comes from your hand. We are foreigners and strangers in your sight, as were all our ancestors. Our days on earth are like a shadow, without hope. LORD our God, all this abundance that we have provided for building you a temple for your

Thanksgiving

Holy Name comes from your hand, and all of it belongs to you. 1 Chronicles 29:10-14

Praise be to the name of God for ever and ever;
    wisdom and power are his.
He changes times and seasons;
    he deposes kings and raises up others.
He gives wisdom to the wise
    and knowledge to the discerning.
He reveals deep and hidden things;
    he knows what lies in darkness,
    and light dwells with him.
I thank and praise you, God of my ancestors:
    You have given me wisdom and power,
you have made known to me what we asked of you.
    Daniel 2:20-23

For Restored Health
Isaiah 38:14-20

The eighth-century BC Judean king, Hezekiah, became deathly ill. He prayed to the Lord to spare him, and God gave him fifteen more years to serve his country. As you read the psalm of praise Hezekiah wrote upon recovery, thank God for the health he has given you and what he has taught you through physical suffering.

> I cried like a swift or thrush,
>> I moaned like a mourning dove.
>
> My eyes grew weak as I looked to the heavens.
>> I am being threatened; Lord, come to my aid!
>
> But what can I say?
>> He has spoken to me, and he himself has done this.
>
> I will walk humbly all my years
>> because of this anguish of my soul.
>
> Lord, by such things people live;
>> and my spirit finds life in them too.
>
> You restored me to health
>> and let me live.
>
> Surely it was for my benefit
>> that I suffered such anguish.
>
> In your love you kept me
>> from the pit of destruction;
>
> you have put all my sins
>> behind your back.
>
> For the grave cannot praise you,
>> death cannot sing your praise;
>
> those who go down to the pit
>> cannot hope for your faithfulness.

Thanksgiving

The living, the living—they praise you,
    as I am doing today;
parents tell their children
    about your faithfulness.
The L<small>ORD</small> will save me,
    and we will sing with stringed instruments
all the days of our lives
    in the temple of the L<small>ORD</small>.

For God's Great Wonders
Psalm 136:1-9, 23-26

The first part of this antiphonal psalm intended for corporate worship thanks God for his acts in creation, each followed by the refrain, "His love endures forever." At the ellipsis the psalmist begins to list specific acts in Israel's history, followed by the refrain. This is a good place for you to list specific things God has done in your community for which you thank him and in the listing remind yourself that his love endures forever.

> Give thanks to the Lord, for he is good.
> > His love endures forever.
>
> Give thanks to the God of gods.
> > His love endures forever.
>
> Give thanks to the Lord of lords:
> > His love endures forever.
>
> to him who alone does great wonders,
> > His love endures forever.
>
> who by his understanding made the heavens,
> > His love endures forever.
>
> who spread out the earth upon the waters,
> > His love endures forever.
>
> who made the great lights —
> > His love endures forever.
>
> the sun to govern the day,
> > His love endures forever.
>
> the moon and stars to govern the night;
> > His love endures forever….
>
> He remembered us in our low estate
> > His love endures forever.
>
> and freed us from our enemies.

Thanksgiving

His love endures forever.
He gives food to every creature.
His love endures forever.
Give thanks to the God of heaven.
His love endures forever. Psalm 136:1-9, 23-26

For Deliverance from sin
Romans 7:21-8:4

Although our sin was forgiven when we trusted Christ, we continue to struggle like the Apostle Paul with the power of that sin and our inability to consistently do what we know is right. Thank God for the victory Christ gives over our sinful nature.

> So I find this law at work: Although I want to do good, evil is right there with me. For in my inner being I delight in God's law; but I see another law at work in me, waging war against the law of my mind and making me a prisoner of the law of sin at work within me. What a wretched man I am! Who will rescue me from this body that is subject to death? Thanks be to God, who delivers me through Jesus Christ our Lord!
> So then, I myself in my mind am a slave to God's law, but in my sinful nature a slave to the law of sin.
> Therefore, there is now no condemnation for those who are in Christ Jesus, because through Christ Jesus the law of the Spirit who gives life has set you free from the law of sin and death. For what the law was powerless to do because it was weakened by the flesh, God did by sending his own Son in the likeness of sinful flesh to be a sin offering. And so he condemned sin in the flesh, in order that the righteous requirement of the law might be fully met in us, who do not live according to the flesh but according to the Spirit.

For Deliverance from Death
1 Corinthians 15: 17-20, 25-26, 50-57

Throughout history people have feared death, but the resurrection of Jesus Christ assures us that physical death is not the end. Thank God for the promise that you too can experience resurrection to a new imperishable body and live forever with him.

> If Christ has not been raised, your faith is futile; you are still in your sins. Then those also who have fallen asleep in Christ are lost. If only for this life we have hope in Christ, we are of all people most to be pitied.
> But Christ has indeed been raised from the dead, the firstfruits of those who have fallen asleep...
>
> He must reign until he has put all his enemies under his feet. The last enemy to be destroyed is death...
>
> I declare to you, brothers and sisters, that flesh and blood cannot inherit the kingdom of God, nor does the perishable inherit the imperishable. Listen, I tell you a mystery: We will not all sleep, but we will all be changed—in a flash, in the twinkling of an eye, at the last trumpet. For the trumpet will sound, the dead will be raised imperishable, and we will be changed. For the perishable must clothe itself with the imperishable, and the mortal with immortality.

Thanksgiving

When the perishable has been clothed with the imperishable, and the mortal with immortality, then the saying that is written will come true:

Death has been swallowed up in victory.

Where, O death, is your victory?
Where, O death, is your sting?

The sting of death is sin, and the power of sin is the law. But thanks be to God! He gives us the victory through our Lord Jesus Christ.

For God's Reign
Revelation 11:17-18

In the last book of the Bible we get a glimpse of heaven where the angels continually praise and thank God. They thank God for taking his great power and beginning to reign even though that means judgement and destruction as well as reward. Join them in thanking God that he will have the final word over evil.

> And the twenty-four elders, who were seated on their thrones before God, fell on their faces and worshiped God, saying:
>
> "We give thanks to you, Lord God Almighty,
>   the One who is and who was,
> because you have taken your great power
>   and have begun to reign.
>
> The nations were angry,
>   and your wrath has come.
>
> The time has come for judging the dead,
>   and for rewarding your servants the prophets
> and your people who revere your name,
>   both great and small —
> and for destroying those who destroy the earth."

Part IV:
Supplication

Supplication

In his model prayer Jesus invited us to ask God to supply our needs.

> Give us today our daily bread. Matthew 5:11

But our prayers should be more than a Christmas list of requests. What God most wants to do in your life is to make you like his Son, Jesus Christ.

> For those God foreknew he also predestined to be conformed to the image of his Son, that he might be the firstborn among many brothers and sisters. Romans 8:29

The following verses will help you to focus each day on some quality that God wants to develop in you. As you meditate on the verses, pray about opportunities to exercise that character trait.

Compassion

Compassion is seeing a need and responding to it from the heart as the Good Samaritan did with the wounded man on the road to Jericho (Luke 10:30-37). Ask God to open your eyes today to see needs around you. He may ask you to show compassion toward someone who has hurt you.

> Blessed are those who have regard for the weak;
>> the Lord delivers them in times of trouble. Psalm 41:1

> Whoever shuts their ears to the cry of the poor
>> will also cry out and not be answered. Proverbs 21:13

> If you do away with the yoke of oppression,
>> with the pointing finger and malicious talk,
> and if you spend yourselves in behalf of the hungry
>> and satisfy the needs of the oppressed,
> then your light will rise in the darkness,
>> and your night will become like the noonday.
>> Isaiah 58:9b-10

> Religion that God our Father accepts as pure and faultless is this: to look after orphans and widows in their distress and to keep oneself from being polluted by the world. James 1:27

> Be kind and compassionate to one another, forgiving each other, just as in Christ God forgave you. Ephesians 4:32

> Do to others as you would have them do to you. Luke 6:31

Supplication

When the Son of Man comes in his glory, and all the angels with him, he will sit on his glorious throne. All the nations will be gathered before him, and he will separate the people one from another as a shepherd separates the sheep from the goats. He will put the sheep on his right and the goats on his left.

Then the King will say to those on his right, 'Come, you who are blessed by my Father; take your inheritance, the kingdom prepared for you since the creation of the world. For I was hungry and you gave me something to eat, I was thirsty and you gave me something to drink, I was a stranger and you invited me in, I needed clothes and you clothed me, I was sick and you looked after me, I was in prison and you came to visit me.'

Then the righteous will answer him, 'Lord, when did we see you hungry and feed you, or thirsty and give you something to drink? When did we see you a stranger and invite you in, or needing clothes and clothe you? When did we see you sick or in prison and go to visit you?'

The King will reply, 'Truly I tell you, whatever you did for one of the least of these brothers and sisters of mine, you did for me.' Matthew 25:31-40

Contentment

It is okay to make our needs known to God, but our consumer society makes us think we "need" all the latest goodies. God desires for us to be content with what he has provided. Thank God for what he has already given you. Ask him to keep you from selfishly going after more and more. Today stop yourself when you are tempted to take more than you need.

> But who are you, a human being, to talk back to God? Shall what is formed say to him who formed it, `Why did you make me like this?' Does not the potter have the right to make out of the same lump of clay some pottery for noble purposes and some for common use? Romans 9:20-21

> Keep falsehood and lies far from me;
>   give me neither poverty nor riches,
>   but give me only my daily bread.
> Otherwise, I may have too much and disown you
>   and say, 'Who is the Lord?'
> Or I may become poor and steal,
>   and so dishonor the name of my God.
>   Proverbs 30:8-9

> I have learned to be content whatever the circumstances. I know what it is to be in need, and I know what it is to have plenty. I have learned the secret of being content in any and every situation, whether well fed or hungry, whether living in plenty or in want. I can do all this through him who gives me strength.
> Philippians 4:11b-13

Supplication

Keep your lives free from the love of money and be content with what you have, because God has said,
> "Never will I leave you;
> never will I forsake you." Hebrews 13:5

Whom have I in heaven but you?
And earth has nothing I desire besides you.
My flesh and my heart may fail,
but God is the strength of my heart
and my portion forever. Psalm 73:25-26

Better is one day in your courts
than a thousand elsewhere;
I would rather be a doorkeeper in the house of my God
than dwell in the tents of the wicked. Psalm 84:10

Then [Jesus] said to them, "Watch out! Be on your guard against all kinds of greed; life does not consist in an abundance of possessions." Luke 12:15

No one can serve two masters. Either you will hate the one and love the other, or you will be devoted to the one and despise the other. You cannot serve both God and money. Matthew 6:24

But godliness with contentment is great gain. For we brought nothing into the world, and we can take nothing out of it. But if we have food and clothing, we will be content with that. Those who want to get rich fall into temptation and a trap and into many foolish and harmful desires that plunge people into ruin and destruction. For the love of money is a root of all kinds of evil. Some people, eager for money, have wandered from the faith and pierced themselves with many griefs. 1 Timothy 6:6-10

Contrition

To be contrite is to be truly sorry for our sin, but pride makes it difficult to admit we are wrong. As you meditate on these verses, seek to have the same attitude that David modeled when he prayed in Psalm 51 after his sin with Bathsheba (2 Samuel 11-12). Today may be a good day to pray through one of the lists in the Confession section of this book.

> "Therefore, you Israelites, I will judge each of you according to your own ways," declares the Sovereign Lord. "Repent! Turn away from all your offenses; then sin will not be your downfall. Rid yourselves of all the offenses you have committed, and get a new heart and a new spirit. Why will you die, people of Israel? For I take no pleasure in the death of anyone," declares the Sovereign Lord. "Repent and live!" Ezekiel 18:30-32

> In repentance and rest is your salvation,
>   in quietness and trust is your strength. Isaiah 30:15b

> Repent then, and turn to God, so that your sins may be wiped out, that times of refreshing may come from the Lord. Acts 3:19

> Because of your stubbornness and your unrepentant heart, you are storing up wrath against yourself for the day of God's wrath, when his righteous judgment will be revealed. Romans 2:5

> Come near to God and he will come near to you. Wash your hands, you sinners, and purify

Supplication

your hearts, you double-minded. Grieve, mourn and wail. Change your laughter to mourning and your joy to gloom. Humble yourselves before the Lord, and he will lift you up. James 4:8-10

For this is what the high and exalted One says—
    he who lives forever, whose name is holy:
"I live in a high and holy place,
    but also with the one who is contrite
        and lowly in spirit,
to revive the spirit of the lowly
    and to revive the heart of the contrite. Isaiah 57:15

If we claim to be without sin, we deceive ourselves and the truth is not in us. If we confess our sins, he is faithful and just and will forgive us our sins and purify us from all unrighteousness. If we claim we have not sinned, we make him out to be a liar and his word is not in us. 1 John 1:8-10

Let us examine our ways and test them,
    and let us return to the Lord.
Let us lift up our hearts and our hands
    to God in heaven, and say:
"We have sinned and rebelled." Lamentations 3:40-42a

Lord, hear my prayer,
    listen to my cry for mercy;
in your faithfulness and righteousness
    come to my relief.
Do not bring your servant into judgment,
    for no one living is righteous before you.
    Psalm 143:1-2

Blessed is the one
    whose transgressions are forgiven,

whose sins are covered.
Blessed is the one
   whose sin the Lord does not count against them
   and in whose spirit is no deceit.
When I kept silent,
   my bones wasted away
   through my groaning all day long.
For day and night
   your hand was heavy on me;
my strength was sapped
   as in the heat of summer.
Then I acknowledged my sin to you
   and did not cover up my iniquity.
I said, "I will confess
   my transgressions to the Lord."
And you forgave
   the guilt of my sin. Psalm 32:1-5

Courage

The courage God wants to see in your life is not risk taking for the sake of an adrenalin rush. It is the trust in him that allows you to step out of your comfort zone for the sake of his kingdom. It may mean standing up when others mock your faith or going to some other country or people group with the gospel, knowing Jesus is with you. Ask God to give you courage today to do what you know is right.

> Be strong and courageous. Do not be afraid or terrified because of them, for the Lord your God goes with you; he will never leave you nor forsake you. Deuteronomy 31:6

> The Lord is my light and my salvation—
>   whom shall I fear?
> The Lord is the stronghold of my life—
>   of whom shall I be afraid? ...
> For in the day of trouble
>   he will keep me safe in his dwelling;
> he will hide me in the shelter of his sacred tent
>   and set me high upon a rock. Psalm 27:1, 5

> Fear of man will prove to be a snare,
>   but whoever trusts in the Lord is kept safe.
>   Proverbs 29:25

> So do not fear, for I am with you;
>   Do not be dismayed, for I am your God.
> I will strengthen you and help you;
>   I will uphold you with my righteous right hand.
>   Isaiah 41:10

You will not fear the terror of night,
    nor the arrow that flies by day.
nor the pestilence that stalks in the darkness,
    nor the plague that destroys at midday.
A thousand may fall at your side,
    ten thousand at your right hand,
    but it will not come near you. Psalm 91:5-7

I, even I, am he who comforts you.
    Who are you that you fear mere mortals,
    human beings who are but grass,
that you forget the LORD your Maker,
    who stretches out the heavens
    and lays the foundations of the earth,
that you live in constant terror every day
    because of the wrath of the oppressor,
    who is bent on destruction?
For where is the wrath of the oppressor? Isaiah 51:12-13

Even though I walk
    through the darkest valley,
I will fear no evil,
    for you are with me;
your rod and your staff,
    they comfort me. Psalm 23:4

We do not belong to those who shrink back and are destroyed, but to those who believe and are saved. Hebrews 10:39

Therefore go and make disciples of all nations, baptizing them in the name of the Father and of the Son and of the Holy Spirit, and teaching them to obey everything I have commanded you. And surely I am with you always, to the very end of the age. Matthew 28:19-20

Supplication

Now, Lord, consider their threats and enable your servants to speak your word with great boldness. Acts 4:29

Pray also for me, that whenever I speak, words may be given me so that I will fearlessly make known the mystery of the gospel, for which I am an ambassador in chains. Pray that I may declare it fearlessly, as I should. Ephesians 6:19-20

Diligence

In our leisure-oriented society it is easy to not put serious effort into things that frankly aren't much fun. Ask God to keep you motivated to work at your job, on your own spiritual growth, in your church, and to reach others for Christ.

> A little sleep, a little slumber,
> > a little folding of the hands to rest—
> and poverty will come on you like a thief
> > and scarcity like an armed man. Proverbs 24:33-34

> Whatever your hand finds to do, do it with all your might, for in the realm of the dead, where you are going, there is neither working nor planning nor knowledge nor wisdom. Ecclesiastes 9:10

> Whatever you do, work at it with all your heart, as working for the Lord, not for human masters, since you know that you will receive an in-heritance from the Lord as a reward. It is the Lord Christ you are serving. Colossians 3.23

> You will seek me and find me when you seek me with all your heart. I will be found by you," declares the Lord. Jeremiah 29:13-14a

> Ask and it will be given to you; seek and you will find; knock and the door will be opened to you. For everyone who asks receives; the one who seeks finds; and to the one who knocks, the door will be opened. Matthew 7:7-8

Supplication

Then [Jesus] said to them all: "Whoever wants to be my disciple must deny themselves and take up their cross daily and follow me. For whoever wants to save their life will lose it, but whoever loses their life for me will save it. What good is it for someone to gain the whole world, and yet lose or forfeit their very self? Luke 9:23-25

But you, man of God, flee from all this [hunger for money], and pursue righteousness, godliness, faith, love, endurance and gentleness. Fight the good fight of the faith. Take hold of the eternal life to which you were called when you made your good confession in the presence of many witnesses. 1 Timothy 6:11-12

Since you are eager to have spiritual gifts, try to excel in gifts that build up the church. 1 Corinthians 14:12b

Always give yourselves fully to the work of the Lord, because you know that your labor in the Lord is not in vain. 1 Corinthians 15:58b

For this very reason, make every effort to
  add to your faith goodness;
    and to goodness, knowledge;
      and to knowledge, self-control;
        and to self-control, perseverance;
          and to perseverance, godliness;
            and to godliness, mutual affection;
              and to mutual affection, love.
For if you possess these qualities in increasing measure, they will keep you from being ineffective and unproductive in your knowledge of our Lord Jesus Christ....

Therefore, my brothers and sisters, make every effort to confirm your calling and election. For if you do these things, you will never stumble, and you will receive a rich welcome into the eternal kingdom of our Lord and Savior Jesus Christ. 2 Peter 1:5-8, 10-11

We remember before our God and Father your work produced by faith, your labor prompted by love, and your endurance inspired by hope in our Lord Jesus Christ. 1 Thessalonians 1:3

So then, dear friends, since you are looking forward to [a new heaven and a new earth, where righteousness dwells], make every effort to be found spotless, blameless and at peace with him. 2 Peter 3:14

Faith

Our faith is not without evidence. (See any good book on apologetics.) But ultimately we must choose to believe, and what we believe will affect the way we live. Ask God to give you confidence in his Word, to get rid of the things in your life that hinder your faith and to show you practical ways of expressing your faith in love.

> In addition to all this, take up the shield of faith, with which you can extinguish all the flaming arrows of the evil one. Ephesians 6:16

> But now apart from the law the righteousness of God has been made known, to which the Law and the Prophets testify. This righteousness is given through faith in Jesus Christ to all who believe. Romans 3:21-22

> What does Scripture say? "Abraham believed God, and it was credited to him as righteousness." ... Therefore, the promise comes by faith, so that it may be by grace and may be guaranteed to all Abraham's offspring—not only to those who are of the law but also to those who have the faith of Abraham. He is the father of us all. Romans 4:3, 16

> Now faith is confidence in what we hope for and assurance about what we do not see. This is what the ancients were commended for.... And without faith it is impossible to please God, because anyone who comes to him must believe

that he exists and that he rewards those who earnestly seek him. Hebrews 11:1-2, 6

All these people were still living by faith when they died. They did not receive the things promised; they only saw them and welcomed them from a distance, admitting that they were foreigners and strangers on earth. People who say such things show that they are looking for a country of their own. If they had been thinking of the country they had left, they would have had opportunity to return. Instead, they were longing for a better country—a heavenly one. Therefore God is not ashamed to be called their God, for he has prepared a city for them. Hebrews 11:13-16

These were all commended for their faith, yet none of them received what had been promised, since God had planned something better for us so that only together with us would they be made perfect. Hebrews 11:39-40

Therefore, since we are surrounded by such a great cloud of witnesses, let us throw off everything that hinders and the sin that so easily entangles. And let us run with perseverance the race marked out for us, fixing our eyes on Jesus, the pioneer and perfecter of faith. For the joy set before him he endured the cross, scorning its shame, and sat down at the right hand of the throne of God. Consider him who endured such opposition from sinners, so that you will not grow weary and lose heart. Hebrews 12:1-3

Faith by itself, if it is not accompanied by action, is dead. James 2:17

Supplication

For in Christ Jesus neither circumcision nor uncircumcision has any value. The only thing that counts is faith expressing itself through love.
Galatians 5:6

Faithfulness

Faithfulness is not doing what God wants once after hearing a sermon on it. It is obedience day after day, month after month, like keeping wedding vows even when you don't feel like it. Ask God to help you today to be faithful in your responsibilities to your family, your employer, your church, and your community.

> This, then, is how you ought to regard us: as servants of Christ and as those entrusted with the mysteries God has revealed. Now it is required that those who have been given a trust must prove faithful. 1 Corinthians 4:1-2

> You must serve faithfully and wholeheartedly in the fear of the LORD. 2 Chronicles 19:9b

> A faithful person will be richly blessed,
>   but one eager to get rich will not go unpunished.
>   Proverbs 28:20

> But from everlasting to everlasting
>   the LORD's love is with those who fear him,
>   and his righteousness with their children's children—
> with those who keep his covenant
>   and remember to obey his precepts. Psalm 103:17-18

> Oh, that my ways were steadfast
>   in obeying your decrees!
> Then I would not be put to shame
>   when I consider all your commands.
>   Psalm 119:5-6

Supplication

How can a young person stay on the path of purity?
   By living according to your word.
I seek you with all my heart;
   do not let me stray from your commands.
I have hidden your word in my heart
   that I might not sin against you. Psalm 119:9-11

'Well done, my good servant!' his master replied. 'Because you have been trustworthy in a very small matter, take charge of ten cities.' Luke 19:17

Finally, be strong in the Lord and in his mighty power. Put on the full armor of God so that you can take your stand against the devil's schemes. For our struggle is not against flesh and blood, but against the rulers, against the authorities, against the powers of this dark world and against the spiritual forces of evil in the heavenly realms. Therefore put on the full armor of God, so that when the day of evil comes, you may be able to stand your ground, and after you have done everything, to stand. Ephesians 6:10-13

I have fought the good fight, I have finished the race, I have kept the faith. Now there is in store for me the crown of righteousness, which the Lord, the righteous Judge, will award to me on that day—and not only to me, but also to all who have longed for his appearing. 2 Timothy 4:7-8

Forgiveness

It's hard to forgive someone who has never apologized, but the opposite of forgiveness is bitterness and resentment that poisons your life and even damages your body. Ask God to show you areas where you are holding on to a wrong that was done you. Turn that pain over to him.

> Forgive us our debts,
>   as we also have forgiven our debtors.
> And lead us not into temptation,
>   but deliver us from the evil one.
>
> For if you forgive other people when they sin against you, your heavenly Father will also forgive you. But if you do not forgive others their sins, your Father will not forgive your sins. Matthew 6:12-15
>
> And when you stand praying, if you hold anything against anyone, forgive them, so that your Father in heaven may forgive you your sins." Mark 11:25
>
> Then Peter came to Jesus and asked, "Lord, how many times shall I forgive my brother or sister who sins against me? Up to seven times?"
> Jesus answered, "I tell you, not seven times, but seventy-seven times. Matthew 18:21-22
>
> "Then the master called the servant in. 'You wicked servant,' he said, 'I canceled all that debt of yours because you begged me to. Shouldn't you have had mercy on your fellow servant just

as I had on you?' In anger his master turned him over to the jailers to be tortured, until he should pay back all he owed.

"This is how my heavenly Father will treat each of you unless you forgive your brother or sister from your heart." Matthew 18:32-35

Be kind and compassionate to one another, forgiving each other, just as in Christ God forgave you. Ephesians 4:32

Therefore, as God's chosen people, holy and dearly loved, clothe yourselves with compassion, kindness, humility, gentleness and patience. Bear with each other and forgive one another if any of you has a grievance against someone. Forgive as the Lord forgave you. And over all these virtues put on love, which binds them all together in perfect unity. Colossians 3:12-14

Generosity

The Old Testament tithe of ten percent is not all that belongs to the Lord. One hundred percent is his. My wealth is not mine to hold onto as if God could not take care of me without a large bank account. It is for me to use as his steward. And it isn't just the use of my money that shows generosity. Do I hoard my time? My privacy? My 'toys'?

> If anyone is poor among your fellow Israelites in any of the towns of the land the LORD your God is giving you, do not be hardhearted or tightfisted toward them. Rather, be openhanded and freely lend them whatever they need. Deuteronomy 15:7-8

Honor the LORD with your wealth,
    with the firstfruits of all your crops;
then your barns will be filled to overflowing,
    and your vats will brim over with new wine.
        Proverbs 3:9-10

Do not withhold good from those to whom it is due,
    when it is in your power to act.
Do not say to your neighbor,
    "Come back tomorrow and I'll give it to you"—
when you already have it with you. Proverbs 3:27-28

> Freely you have received, freely give. Matthew 10:8b

A generous person will prosper;
    whoever refreshes others will be refreshed.
        Proverbs 11:25

Supplication

Give, and it will be given to you. A good measure, pressed down, shaken together and running over, will be poured into your lap. For with the measure you use, it will be measured to you." Luke 6:38

But since you excel in everything—in faith, in speech, in knowledge, in complete earnestness and in the love we have kindled in you—see that you also excel in this grace of giving. 2 Corinthians 8:7

For if the willingness is there, the gift is acceptable according to what one has, not according to what one does not have. Our desire is not that others might be relieved while you are hard pressed, but that there might be equality. At the present time your plenty will supply what they need, so that in turn their plenty will supply what you need. The goal is equality. 2 Corinthians 8:12-14

Remember this: Whoever sows sparingly will also reap sparingly, and whoever sows generously will also reap generously. Each of you should give what you have decided in your heart to give, not reluctantly or under compulsion, for God loves a cheerful giver. And God is able to bless you abundantly, so that in all things at all times, having all that you need, you will abound in every good work... You will be enriched in every way so that you can be generous on every occasion, and through us your generosity will result in thanksgiving to God.
This service that you perform is not only supplying the needs of the Lord's people but is

also overflowing in many expressions of thanks to God. 2 Corinthians 9:6-8, 11-12

Command those who are rich in this present world not to be arrogant nor to put their hope in wealth, which is so uncertain, but to put their hope in God, who richly provides us with everything for our enjoyment. Command them to do good, to be rich in good deeds, and to be generous and willing to share. In this way they will lay up treasure for themselves as a firm foundation for the coming age, so that they may take hold of the life that is truly life. 1 Timothy 6:17-19

Goodness

Our goodness is a reflection of God's goodness, which is always active, doing something for others. Ask God to make his goodness overflow to others through you today.

> Is not this the kind of fasting I have chosen:
> to loose the chains of injustice
>   and untie the cords of the yoke,
> to set the oppressed free
>   and break every yoke?
> Is it not to share your food with the hungry
>   and to provide the poor wanderer with shelter—
> when you see the naked, to clothe them,
>   and not to turn away from your own flesh and blood? Isaiah 58:6-7

> If your enemy is hungry, give him food to eat;
>   if he is thirsty, give him water to drink.
> In doing this, you will heap burning coals on his head,
>   and the LORD will reward you. Proverbs 25:21-22

> Make sure that nobody pays back wrong for wrong, but always strive to do what is good for each other and for everyone else. 1 Thessalonians 5:15

> You have heard that it was said, 'Eye for eye, and tooth for tooth.' But I tell you, do not resist an evil person. If anyone slaps you on the right cheek, turn to them the other cheek also. And if anyone wants to sue you and take your shirt, hand over your coat as well. If anyone forces you to go one mile, go with

them two miles. Give to the one who asks you, and do not turn away from the one who wants to borrow from you. Matthew 5:38-42

Let us not become weary in doing good, for at the proper time we will reap a harvest if we do not give up. Therefore, as we have opportunity, let us do good to all people, especially to those who belong to the family of believers. Galatians 6:9-10

Your beauty should not come from outward adornment, such as elaborate hairstyles and the wearing of gold jewelry or fine clothes. Rather, it should be that of your inner self, the unfading beauty of a gentle and quiet spirit, which is of great worth in God's sight. 1 Peter 3:3-4

This is a trustworthy saying. And I want you to stress these things, so that those who have trusted in God may be careful to devote themselves to doing what is good. These things are excellent and profitable for everyone. Titus 3:8

May our Lord Jesus Christ himself and God our Father, who loved us and by his grace gave us eternal encouragement and good hope, encourage your hearts and strengthen you in every good deed and word. 2 Thessalonians 2:16-17

Gratitude

Gratitude is an attitude that recognizes that what I have is a gift from God. To deny that truth is to pretend to be God. Ask God to make you conscious at every moment of how much you owe him. Think of people God has used to bless you and ways that you can show your appreciation to them today.

For although they knew God, they neither glorified him as God nor gave thanks to him, but their thinking became futile and their foolish hearts were darkened. Romans 1:21

When you have eaten and are satisfied, praise the LORD your God for the good land he has given you. Be careful that you do not forget the LORD your God,… But remember the LORD your God, for it is he who gives you the ability to produce wealth, and so confirms his covenant, which he swore to your ancestors, as it is today. Deuteronomy 8:10-11a, 18

For everything God created is good, and nothing is to be rejected if it is received with thanksgiving, because it is consecrated by the word of God and prayer. 1 Timothy 4:4

Those who sacrifice thank offerings honor me,
    and to the blameless I will show my salvation.
    Psalm 50:23

Enter his gates with thanksgiving
    and his courts with praise;

give thanks to him and praise his name.
For the L ORD is good and his love endures forever;
    his faithfulness continues through all generations.
    Psalm 100:4

Give thanks to the L ORD, for he is good;
    his love endures forever.
Let the redeemed of the L ORD tell their story—
    those he redeemed from the land of the foe,…

Let them give thanks to the L ORD for his unfailing love
    and his wonderful deeds for mankind.
Let them sacrifice thank offerings
    and tell of his works with songs of joy.
    Psalm 107:1-2, 21-22

It is good to praise the L ORD
    and make music to your name, O Most High,
to proclaim your love in the morning
    and your faithfulness at night,
to the music of the ten-stringed lyre
    and the melody of the harp. Psalm 92:1-3

Devote yourselves to prayer, being watchful and thankful. Colossians 4:2

…giving joyful thanks to the Father, who has qualified you to share in the inheritance of his holy people in the kingdom of light. Colossians 1:12

Sing and make music in your heart to the Lord, always giving thanks to God the Father for everything, in the name of our Lord Jesus Christ.
Ephesians 5:19b-20

Holiness

Holiness means being set apart for God's use, different from the ordinary, not to be treated casually. If you belong to God, you are special and should treat yourself, not as better than others, but as reserved for the King's use. As you read these verses, commit yourself to live as one set apart to God.

> I am the LORD, who brought you up out of
> Egypt to be your God; therefore be holy,
> because I am holy. Leviticus 11:45

> Praise be to the LORD, the God of Israel,
>   because he has come to his people
>   and redeemed them.
> He has raised up a horn of salvation for us
>   in the house of his servant David...
> to enable us to serve him without fear
>   in holiness and righteousness before him
>   all our days. Luke 1:68-69, 74b-75

Husbands, love your wives, just as Christ loved the church and gave himself up for her to make her holy, cleansing her by the washing with water through the word, and to present her to himself as a radiant church, without stain or wrinkle or any other blemish, but holy and blameless. Ephesians 5:25-27

You also, like living stones, are being built into a spiritual house to be a holy priesthood, offering spiritual sacrifices acceptable to God through Jesus Christ...You are a chosen people, a royal priesthood, a holy nation, God's special possession, that you may declare the praises of him who called you out of darkness into his wonderful light. 1 Peter 2:5, 9

In a large house there are articles not only of gold and silver, but also of wood and clay; some are for special purposes and some for common use. Those who cleanse themselves from the latter will be instruments for special purposes, made holy, useful to the Master and prepared to do any good work. 2 Timothy 2:20-21

You ought to live holy and godly lives as you look forward to the day of God and speed its coming. 2 Peter 3:11b-12a

It is God's will that you should be sanctified: that you should avoid sexual immorality; that each of you should learn to control his own body in a way that is holy and honorable, not in passionate lust like the pagans, who do not know God;... For God did not call us to be impure, but to live a holy life. 1 Thessalonians 4:3-5, 7

Make every effort to live in peace with everyone and to be holy; without holiness no one will see the Lord. Hebrews 12:14

As obedient children, do not conform to the evil desires you had when you lived in ignorance. But just as he who called you is holy, so be holy in all you do; for it is written: "Be holy, because I am holy." 1 Peter 1:14-16

Humility

The humility God wants to see in you comes, not from a poor self-image, but from knowing exactly who you are as his loved child. With this kind of humility you can take the lowest place without being demeaned or the highest place without others feeling put down. As you meditate on these verses, think about how you can imitate Jesus' attitude of serving today.

> Humble yourselves before the Lord, and he will lift you up. James 4:10

> If my people, who are called by my name, will humble themselves and pray and seek my face and turn from their wicked ways, then will I hear from heaven and will forgive their sin and will heal their land. 2 Chronicles 7:14

> For those who exalt themselves will be humbled, and those who humble themselves will be exalted. Matthew 23:12

> All of you, clothe yourselves with humility toward one another, because,
> > "God opposes the proud
> > but gives grace to the humble." 1 Peter 5:5b-6

> Blessed are the meek,
> > for they will inherit the earth. Matthew 5:5

> In your relationships with one another, have the same mindset as Christ Jesus:

Who, being in very nature God,
  did not consider equality with God something
to be used to his own advantage;
rather, he made himself nothing
  by taking the very nature of a servant,
  being made in human likeness.
And being found in appearance as a man,
  he humbled himself
  by becoming obedient to death —
    even death on a cross! Philippians 2:5-7

When [Jesus] had finished washing their feet, he put on his clothes and returned to his place. "Do you understand what I have done for you?" he asked them. "You call me 'Teacher' and 'Lord,' and rightly so, for that is what I am. Now that I, your Lord and Teacher, have washed your feet, you also should wash one another's feet. I have set you an example that you should do as I have done for you." John 13:12-15

Whoever wants to become great among you must be your servant, and whoever wants to be first must be slave of all. For even the Son of Man did not come to be served, but to serve, and to give his life as a ransom for many. Mark 10:43b-45

[Jesus] said to me, "My grace is sufficient for you, for my power is made perfect in weakness." Therefore I will boast all the more gladly about my weaknesses, so that Christ's power may rest on me. That is why, for Christ's sake, I delight in weaknesses, in insults, in hardships, in persecutions, in difficulties. For when I am weak, then I am strong. 2 Corinthians 12:9-10

Supplication

For by the grace given me I say to every one of you: Do not think of yourself more highly than you ought, but rather think of yourself with sober judgment, in accordance with the faith God has distributed to each of you. For just as each of us has one body with many members, and these members do not all have the same function, so in Christ we, though many, form one body, and each member belongs to all the others. Romans 12:3-5

Integrity

Integrity means that what I do is consistent with what I say. God isn't impressed by the hypocrisy of going through religious motions. He looks for a real heart change that works itself out in justice, mercy and humility. (Study the book of James if you need specifics.) The result is a reputation that inspires confidence and trust. Talk to the Lord today about ways in which your choices may be inconsistent with the faith you profess.

> Whoever walks in integrity walks securely,
> > but whoever takes crooked paths will be found out.
> > Proverbs 10:9

> The integrity of the upright guides them,
> > but the unfaithful are destroyed by their duplicity.
> > Proverbs 11:3

> A good name is more desirable than great riches;
> > to be esteemed is better than silver or gold.
> > Proverbs 22:1

> Be careful not to practice your righteousness in front of others to be seen by them. If you do, you will have no reward from your Father in heaven. Matthew 6:1

> Will the Lord be pleased with thousands of rams,
> > with ten thousand rivers of olive oil?
> Shall I offer my firstborn for my transgression,
> > the fruit of my body for the sin of my soul?
> He has shown you, O mortal, what is good.
> > And what does the Lord require of you?

Supplication

To act justly and to love mercy
   And to walk humbly with your God. Micah 6:7-8

For I desire mercy, not sacrifice,
   and acknowledgment of God
      rather than burnt offerings. Hosea 6:6

When you make a vow to God, do not delay to fulfill it. He has no pleasure in fools; fulfill your vow. It is better not to make a vow than to make one and not fulfill it. Do not let your mouth lead you into sin. And do not protest to the temple messenger, "My vow was a mistake." Why should God be angry at what you say and destroy the work of your hands? Ecclesiastes 5:4-6

Teach slaves to be subject to their masters in everything, to try to please them, not to talk back to them, and not to steal from them, but to show that they can be fully trusted, so that in every way they will make the teaching about God our Savior attractive. Titus 2:9

I tell you, do not swear an oath at all... All you need to say is simply 'Yes' or 'No'; anything beyond this comes from the evil one. Matthew 5:34a, 37

Your beauty should not come from outward adornment, such as elaborate hairstyles and the wearing of gold jewelry or fine clothes. Rather, it should be that of your inner self, the unfading beauty of a gentle and quiet spirit, which is of great worth in God's sight. 1 Peter 3:3-4

Joy

Joy does not depend on circumstances the way happiness does. True joy is much deeper. It comes out of an enduring relationship with a loving God, walking with him in obedience even when you can't see immediate results. Ask God to help you to see beyond today's problems to his unchanging love and to experience the joy of knowing and walking with him.

> Our mouths were filled with laughter,
> > our tongues with songs of joy.
>
> Then it was said among the nations,
> > "The Lord has done great things for them."
>
> The Lord has done great things for us,
> > and we are filled with joy. Psalm 126:2-3

> Though the fig tree does not bud
> > and there are no grapes on the vines,
>
> though the olive crop fails
> > and the fields produce no food,
>
> though there are no sheep in the pen
> > and no cattle in the stalls,
>
> yet I will rejoice in the Lord,
> > I will be joyful in God my Savior.
>
> The Sovereign Lord is my strength;
> > he makes my feet like the feet of a deer,
> > he enables me to go on the heights. Habakkuk 3:17-19

> Sing the praises of the Lord, you his faithful people;
> > praise his holy name.
>
> For his anger lasts only a moment,
> > but his favor lasts a lifetime;

Supplication

weeping may remain for a night,
    but rejoicing comes in the morning...
You turned my wailing into dancing;
    you removed my sackcloth and clothed me with joy,
that my heart may sing your praises and not be silent.
    LORD my God, I will praise you forever.
    Psalm 30:4-5, 11-12

Shouts of joy and victory resound
    in the tents of the righteous:
"The LORD's right hand has done mighty things!"
    Psalm 118:15

You make known to me the path of life;
    you will fill me with joy in your presence,
    with eternal pleasures at your right hand.
    Psalm 16:11

If you obey my commands, you will remain in my love, just as I have kept my Father's commands and remain in his love. I have told you this so that my joy may be in you and that your joy may be complete. John 15:10-11

Though you have not seen him, you love him; and even though you do not see him now, you believe in him and are filled with an inexpressible and glorious joy, for you are receiving the end result of your faith, the salvation of your souls. 1 Peter 1:8-9

Rejoice in the Lord always. I will say it again: Rejoice! Philippians 4:4

Kindness

You know what kindness is—it's the way you would like other people to treat you. It requires noticing needs and being willing to interrupt your own agenda to meet them. Ask God to open your eyes to see and your heart to feel as he does. Then actively look for ways to show kindness today.

> Be kind and compassionate to one another, forgiving each other, just as in Christ God forgave you. Ephesians 4:32

> Therefore, as we have opportunity, let us do good to all people, especially to those who belong to the family of believers. Galatians 6:10

> Love your enemies, do good to them, and lend to them without expecting to get anything back. Then your reward will be great, and you will be children of the Most High, because he is kind to the ungrateful and wicked. Luke 6:35

If your enemy is hungry, give him food to eat;
   if he is thirsty, give him water to drink.
In doing this, you will heap burning coals on his head,
   and the Lord will reward you. Proverbs 25:21-22

> Do to others as you would have them do to you. If you love those who love you, what credit is that to you? Even sinners love those who love them. And if you do good to those who are good to you, what credit is that to you? Even sinners do that. And if you lend to those from whom you

expect repayment, what credit is that to you? Even sinners lend to sinners, expecting to be repaid in full.

But love your enemies, do good to them, and lend to them without expecting to get anything back. Then your reward will be great, and you will be children of the Most High, because he is kind to the ungrateful and wicked. Be merciful, just as your Father is merciful. Luke 6:31-36

So when you give to the needy, do not announce it with trumpets, as the hypocrites do in the synagogues and on the streets, to be honored by others. Truly I tell you, they have received their reward in full. But when you give to the needy, do not let your left hand know what your right hand is doing, so that your giving may be in secret. Then your Father, who sees what is done in secret, will reward you. Matthew 6:2-4

Love

Love is an attitude that permeates everything we do, or its lack sucks the meaning from the most self-sacrificing action. Examine your relationships with the people you will encounter today, and ask God to give you the kind of love described in 1 Corinthians 13.

'Love the Lord your God with all your heart and with all your soul and with all your mind.' This is the first and greatest commandment. And the second is like it: 'Love your neighbor as yourself.' All the Law and the Prophets hang on these two commandments. Matthew 22:37-40

Dear children, let us not love with words or tongue but with actions and in truth. 1 John 3:18

Dear friends, let us love one another, for love comes from God. Everyone who loves has been born of God and knows God. Whoever does not love does not know God, because God is love.... Dear friends, since God so loved us, we also ought to love one another. 1 John 4:7, 11

If I speak in the tongues of men or of angels,
    but do not have love,
I am only a resounding gong
    or a clanging cymbal.

If I have the gift of prophecy
    and can fathom all mysteries
        and all knowledge,
    and if I have a faith that can move mountains,

Supplication

but do not have love,
   I am nothing.

If I give all I possess to the poor
   and give over my body to hardship that I may boast,
but do not have love,
   I gain nothing.

Love is patient,
   love is kind.

It does not envy,
   it does not boast,
      it is not proud.
It does not dishonor others,
   it is not self-seeking,
      it is not easily angered,
         it keeps no record of wrongs.

Love does not delight in evil
   but rejoices with the truth.

It always protects,
   always trusts,
      always hopes,
         always perseveres.

Love never fails...

And now these three remain:
   faith, hope and love.
But the greatest of these is love. I Corinthians 13:1-8a, 13

Obedience

What did you hear in church last Sunday or read in your devotions this morning that you need to put into practice? God isn't content with our going through the motions of being religious. He wants obedience. This may be a good day to pray through one of the lists of sins under Confession in this book.

> Hear, Israel, and be careful to obey so that it may go well with you and that you may increase greatly in a land flowing with milk and honey, just as the LORD, the God of your fathers, promised you. Deuteronomy 6:3

> Now what I am commanding you today is not too difficult for you or beyond your reach…No, the word is very near you; it is in your mouth and in your heart so you may obey it. Deuteronomy 30:11, 14

> Does the LORD delight in burnt offerings and sacrifices
>   as much as in obeying the LORD?
> To obey is better than sacrifice,
>   and to heed is better than the fat of rams.
> 1 Samuel 15:22

> Not everyone who says to me, 'Lord, Lord,' will enter the kingdom of heaven, but only the one who does the will of my Father who is in heaven. Matthew 7:21

> Do not merely listen to the word, and so deceive yourselves. Do what it says. James 1:22

Supplication

Whatever you have learned or received or heard from me, or seen in me—put it into practice. And the God of peace will be with you. Philippians 4:9

You have laid down precepts
    that are to be fully obeyed.
Oh, that my ways were steadfast
    in obeying your decrees!
Then I would not be put to shame
    when I consider all your commands. Psalm 119:4-6

Therefore everyone who hears these words of mine and puts them into practice is like a wise man who built his house on the rock. The rain came down, the streams rose, and the winds blew and beat against that house; yet it did not fall, because it had its foundation on the rock. But everyone who hears these words of mine and does not put them into practice is like a foolish man who built his house on sand. The rain came down, the streams rose, and the winds blew and beat against that house, and it fell with a great crash. Matthew 7:24-27

If you love me, keep my commands. John 14:15

Patience

In a world of e-mail and microwaves we are used to instant solutions. It is hard to wait on God's timing and not to become irritated with other people's foibles. As you pray these verses, remind yourself who God is, what he has done for you in the past and how wonderful it will be when we get to heaven.

Wait for the LORD;
    be strong and take heart
and wait for the LORD. Psalm 27:14

I waited patiently for the LORD;
    he turned to me and heard my cry. Psalm 40:1

I wait for the LORD, my soul waits,
    and in his word I put my hope.
My soul waits for the Lord
    more than watchmen wait for the morning,
    more than watchmen wait for the morning.
Psalm 130:5-6

Better a patient person than a warrior,
    one with self-control than one who takes a city.
Proverbs 16:32

A person's wisdom yields patience;
    it is to one's glory to overlook an offense.
Proverbs 19:11

The end of a matter is better than its beginning,
    and patience is better than pride.
Ecclesiastes 7:8

Supplication

Yes, Lord, walking in the way of your laws,
    we wait for you;
your name and renown
    are the desire of our hearts. Isaiah 26:8

Then the Lord replied:
"Write down the revelation
    and make it plain on tablets
    so that a herald may run with it.
For the revelation awaits an appointed time;
    it speaks of the end and will not prove false.
Though it linger, wait for it;
    It will certainly come and will not delay.
Habakkuk 2:2-3

Even youths grow tired and weary,
    and young men stumble and fall;
but those who hope in the Lord
    will renew their strength.
They will soar on wings like eagles;
    they will run and not grow weary,
    they will walk and not be faint. Isaiah 40: 30-31

Peace

Peace is both a quality in the believer and an attitude that spills out to others. It comes from trusting God, making his agenda your own and doing all you can to promote peace with others. Rest in that peace today and look for ways to share it.

> Take my yoke upon you and learn from me, for I am gentle and humble in heart, and you will find rest for your souls. For my yoke is easy and my burden is light. Matthew 11:29-30

> Peace I leave with you; my peace I give you. I do not give to you as the world gives. Do not let your hearts be troubled and do not be afraid. John 14:27

> I have told you these things, so that in me you may have peace. In this world you will have trouble. But take heart! I have overcome the world. John 16:33

> Do not be anxious about anything, but in every situation, by prayer and petition, with thanksgiving, present your requests to God. And the peace of God, which transcends all understanding, will guard your hearts and your minds in Christ Jesus. Philippians 4:6-7

> No discipline seems pleasant at the time, but painful. Later on, however, it produces a harvest of righteousness and peace for those who have been trained by it. Hebrews 12:11

Supplication

May God himself, the God of peace, sanctify you through and through. May your whole spirit, soul and body be kept blameless at the coming of our Lord Jesus Christ. 1 Thessalonians 5:23

Blessed are the peacemakers,
    for they will be called children of God. Matthew 5:9

If it is possible, as far as it depends on you, live at peace with everyone. Romans 12:18

Peacemakers who sow in peace raise a harvest of righteousness. James 3:18

A gentle answer turns away wrath,
    but a harsh word stirs up anger...
A hot-tempered person stirs up dissension,
    but the one who is patient calms a quarrel.
Proverbs 15:1, 18

For he himself is our peace, who has made the two groups one and has destroyed the barrier, the dividing wall of hostility, by setting aside in his flesh the law with its commands and regulations. His purpose was to create in himself one new humanity out of the two, thus making peace, and in one body to reconcile both of them to God through the cross, by which he put to death their hostility. He came and preached peace to you who were far away and peace to those who were near. For through him we both have access to the Father by one Spirit. Ephesians 2:14-18

Perseverance

Perseverance means sticking to it when the going gets rough. Life is a marathon, not a sprint. As you pray these verses, ask God to use the problems in your life to make you a more mature and complete person.

Consider it pure joy, my brothers and sisters, whenever you face trials of many kinds, because you know that the testing of your faith produces perseverance. Let perseverance finish its work so that you may be mature and complete, not lacking anything. James 1:2-4

Be patient, then, brothers and sisters, until the Lord's coming. See how the farmer waits for the land to yield its valuable crop, patiently waiting for the autumn and spring rains. You too, be patient and stand firm, because the Lord's coming is near. Don't grumble against one another, brothers and sisters, or you will be judged. The Judge is standing at the door!
Brothers and sisters, as an example of patience in the face of suffering, take the prophets who spoke in the name of the Lord. As you know, we count as blessed those who have persevered. You have heard of Job's perseverance and have seen what the Lord finally brought about. The Lord is full of compassion and mercy. James 5:7-11

I consider that our present sufferings are not worth comparing with the glory that will be revealed in us. Romans 8:18

Supplication

And we know that in all things God works for the good of those who love him, who have been called according to his purpose. Romans 8:28

Consider him who endured such opposition from sinners, so that you will not grow weary and lose heart. Hebrews 12:3

You need to persevere so that when you have done the will of God, you will receive what he has promised. For,

"In just a little while,
    he who is coming will come
and will not delay." Hebrews 10:36-37

Therefore I endure everything for the sake of the elect, that they too may obtain the salvation that is in Christ Jesus, with eternal glory. Here is a trustworthy saying:

If we died with him,
    we will also live with him;
if we endure,
    we will also reign with him. 2 Timothy 2:10-12a

Therefore we do not lose heart. Though outwardly we are wasting away, yet inwardly we are being renewed day by day. For our light and momentary troubles are achieving for us an eternal glory that far outweighs them all. So we fix our eyes not on what is seen, but on what is unseen. For what is seen is temporary, but what is unseen is eternal. 2 Corinthians 4:16-18

Purity

While holiness has the idea of separation for God, purity ensures that what is separated is unadulterated, unpolluted. Ask God to help you to avoid people, places, and habits—maybe even popular music or TV shows—that would water down or pollute your commitment to him.

> Blessed are the pure in heart,
>   for they will see God. Matthew 5:8

> Flee the evil desires of youth, and pursue righteousness, faith, love and peace, along with those who call on the Lord out of a pure heart. 2 Timothy 2:22

> Those who consider themselves religious and yet do not keep a tight rein on their tongues deceive themselves, and their religion is worthless. Religion that God our Father accepts as pure and faultless is this: to look after orphans and widows in their distress and to keep oneself from being polluted by the world. James 1:26-27

> Come near to God and he will come near to you. Wash your hands, you sinners, and purify your hearts, you double-minded. James 4:8

> Do you not know that your body is a temple of the Holy Spirit, who is in you, whom you have received from God? You are not your own; you were bought at a price. Therefore honor God with your body. 1 Corinthians 6:19-20

Supplication

Since we have these promises, dear friends, let us purify ourselves from everything that contaminates body and spirit, perfecting holiness out of reverence for God. 2 Corinthians 7:1

What shall we say, then? Shall we go on sinning so that grace may increase? By no means! We are those who have died to sin; how can we live in it any longer?... But now that you have been set free from sin and have become slaves to God, the benefit you reap leads to holiness, and the result is eternal life. Romans 6:1-2, 22

Do not conform to the pattern of this world, but be transformed by the renewing of your mind. Romans 12:2a

Since, then, you have been raised with Christ, set your hearts on things above, where Christ is seated at the right hand of God. Set your minds on things above, not on earthly things. Colossians 3:1-2

Finally, brothers and sisters, whatever is true, whatever is noble, whatever is right, whatever is pure, whatever is lovely, whatever is admirable—if anything is excellent or praiseworthy—think about such things. Philippians 4:8

May God himself, the God of peace, sanctify you through and through. May your whole spirit, soul and body be kept blameless at the coming of our Lord Jesus Christ. 1 Thessalonians 5:23

Righteousness

Righteousness is the quality of consistently choosing what is right. We are not saved by the good things we do, but God saved us so that we would be able to choose the good as he does. Ask God to make you want to do right as much as you want a cold drink on a hot day or a good dinner after a hard day's work.

> Blessed are those who hunger and thirst for righteousness, for they will be filled. Matthew 5:6

> I thirst for you like a parched land. Psalm 143:6b

> The fruit of righteousness will be peace;
> > its effect will be quietness and confidence forever. Isaiah 32:17

> But now apart from the law the righteousness of God has been made known, to which the Law and the Prophets testify. This righteousness is given through faith in Jesus Christ to all who believe. Romans 3:21-22a

> For it is by grace you have been saved, through faith—and this not from yourselves, it is the gift of God—not by works, so that no one can boast. For we are God's handiwork, created in Christ Jesus to do good works, which God prepared in advance for us to do. Ephesians 2:8-10

> Blessed is the one
> > who does not walk in step with the wicked
> > > or stand in the way that sinners take

Supplication

    or sit in the company of mockers,
but whose delight is in the law of the LORD,
    and who meditates on his law day and night.
That person is like a tree planted by streams of water,
    which yields its fruit in season
and whose leaf does not wither—
whatever they do prospers. Psalm 1:1-3

The fruit of the righteous is a tree of life,
    and the one who is wise saves lives. Proverbs 11:30

Self-control

Often the choices we make seem insignificant, but they add up to someone or something controlling our lives. Who controls your choices—peers, advertisers, the Holy Spirit? Alcohol, drugs and tobacco can easily get control. So can anger, sex, junk food and credit cards. Self-control means being conscious of your choices in the light of Jesus' return. Ask the Holy Spirit to help you today to choose wisely.

> Like a city whose walls are broken through
> is a person who lacks self-control. Proverbs 25:28

> You have heard that it was said, `Eye for eye, and tooth for tooth.' But I tell you, do not resist an evil person. If anyone strikes you on the right cheek, turn to them the other cheek also. Matthew 5:38-39

> Let us not be like others, who are asleep, but let us be awake and sober. For those who sleep, sleep at night, and those who get drunk, get drunk at night. But since we belong to the day, let us be sober, putting on faith and love as a breastplate, and the hope of salvation as a helmet. 1 Thessalonians 5:6-8

> For the grace of God has appeared that offers salvation to all people. It teaches us to say "No" to ungodliness and worldly passions, and to live self-controlled, upright and godly lives in this present age, while we wait for the blessed hope—the appearing of the glory of our great God and Savior, Jesus Christ, who gave himself

Supplication

for us to redeem us from all wickedness and to purify for himself a people that are his very own, eager to do what is good. Titus 2:11-14

"I have the right to do anything," you say—but not everything is beneficial. "I have the right to do anything"—but I will not be mastered by anything. 1 Corinthians 6:12

We take captive every thought to make it obedient to Christ. 2 Corinthians 10:5b

My dear brothers and sisters, take note of this: Everyone should be quick to listen, slow to speak and slow to become angry, because human anger does not produce the righteousness that God desires. James 1:19-20

With the tongue we praise our Lord and Father, and with it we curse human beings, who have been made in God's likeness. Out of the same mouth come praise and cursing. My brothers and sisters, this should not be. James 3:9-10

With minds that are alert and fully sober, set your hope on the grace to be brought to you when Jesus Christ is revealed at his coming. 1 Peter 1:13

Be alert and of sober mind. Your enemy the devil prowls around like a roaring lion looking for someone to devour. Resist him, standing firm in the faith, because you know that the family of believers throughout the world is undergoing the same kind of sufferings. 1 Peter 5:8-9

Self-denial

Our self-centered society asks constantly, "What's in it for me?" Self-denial sets aside what I want, to choose what God wants instead. Ask the Holy Spirit to point out areas in which you should be denying yourself to choose something of greater value.

> Then Jesus said to his disciples, "Whoever wants to be my disciple must deny themselves and take up their cross and follow me. For whoever wants to save their life will lose it, but whoever loses their life for me will find it." Matthew 16:24-25

> If anyone comes to me and does not hate father and mother, wife and children, brothers and sisters—yes, even their own life—such a person cannot be my disciple. Luke 14:26

> "Truly I tell you," Jesus said to them, "no one who has left home or wife or brothers or sisters or parents or children for the sake of the kingdom of God will fail to receive many times as much in this age, and in the age to come eternal life." Luke 18:29-30

> If your right eye causes you to sin, gouge it out and throw it away. It is better for you to lose one part of your body than for your whole body to be thrown into hell. And if your right hand causes you to stumble, cut it off and throw it away. It is better for you to lose one part of your body than for your whole body to go into hell. Matthew 5:29

Supplication

Therefore I do not run like someone running aimlessly; I do not fight like a boxer beating the air. No, I strike a blow to my body and make it my slave so that after I have preached to others, I myself will not be disqualified for the prize. 1 Corinthians 9:26-27

For to me, to live is Christ and to die is gain. Philippians 1:21

We who are strong ought to bear with the failings of the weak and not to please ourselves. Romans 15:1

He himself bore our sins in his body on the cross, so that we might die to sins and live for righteousness. 1 Peter 2:24a

Those who belong to Christ Jesus have crucified the flesh with its passions and desires. Galatians 5:24

Put to death, therefore, whatever belongs to your earthly nature: sexual immorality, impurity, lust, evil desires and greed, which is idolatry. Colossians 3:5

For we know that our old self was crucified with him so that the body ruled by sin might be done away with, that we should no longer be slaves to sin—because anyone who has died has been set free from sin.
Now if we died with Christ, we believe that we will also live with him. For we know that since Christ was raised from the dead, he cannot die

again; death no longer has mastery over him. The death he died, he died to sin once for all; but the life he lives, he lives to God.

In the same way, count yourselves dead to sin but alive to God in Christ Jesus. Romans 6:6-11

For if you live according to the flesh, you will die; but if by the Spirit you put to death the misdeeds of the body, you will live. For those who are led by the Spirit of God are the children of God. Romans 8:13-14

Submission

Submission is not a popular word in a society that values independence and individuality. Submission means putting someone else's agenda ahead of your own. Ask God to show you where your independent spirit with family members or those in authority is bringing criticism on Christ.

> Submit yourselves for the Lord's sake to every human authority: whether to the emperor, as the supreme authority, or to governors, who are sent by him to punish those who do wrong and to commend those who do right. For it is God's will that by doing good you should silence the ignorant talk of foolish people. Live as free people, but do not use your freedom as a cover-up for evil; live as God's slaves. 1 Peter 2:13-16

> Let everyone be subject to the governing authorities, for there is no authority except that which God has established. The authorities that exist have been established by God. Consequently, whoever rebels against the authority is rebelling against what God has instituted, and those who do so will bring judgment on themselves... Give to everyone what you owe them: If you owe taxes, pay taxes; if revenue, then revenue; if respect, then respect; if honor, then honor. Romans 13:1-2, 7

> Remind the people to be subject to rulers and authorities, to be obedient, to be ready to do whatever is good. Titus 3:1

To the elders among you, I appeal as a fellow elder and a witness of Christ's sufferings who also will share in the glory to be revealed: Be shepherds of God's flock that is under your care, watching over them—not because you must, but because you are willing, as God wants you to be; not pursuing dishonest gain, but eager to serve; not lording it over those entrusted to you, but being examples to the flock... In the same way, you who are younger, submit yourselves to your elders. All of you, clothe yourselves with humility toward one another, because,

"God opposes the proud
   but shows favor to the humble." 1 Peter 5:1-3, 5a

Submit to one another out of reverence for Christ.
Wives, submit yourselves to your own husbands as you do to the Lord...
Husbands, love your wives, just as Christ loved the church and gave himself up for her...
Children, obey your parents in the Lord, for this is right...
Fathers, do not exasperate your children; instead, bring them up in the training and instruction of the Lord...
Slaves, obey your earthly masters with respect and fear, and with sincerity of heart, just as you would obey Christ...
And masters, treat your slaves in the same way... Ephesians 5:21, 22, 25; 6:1, 4, 5, 9a

Be careful, however, that the exercise of your rights does not become a stumbling block to the

Supplication

weak... Though I am free and belong to no one, I have made myself a slave to everyone, to win as many as possible. To the Jews I became like a Jew, to win the Jews. To those under the law I became like one under the law (though I myself am not under the law), so as to win those under the law. To those not having the law I became like one not having the law (though I am not free from God's law but am under Christ's law), so as to win those not having the law. To the weak I became weak, to win the weak. I have become all things to all people so that by all possible means I might save some. I do all this for the sake of the gospel, that I may share in its blessings. 1 Corinthians 8:9, 9:19-23

Trust

Trust is putting your faith into action in a concrete situation. As you pray these verses, consciously rest in God and give him your present situation with confidence regardless of how hopeless circumstances may appear.

Trust in the Lord with all your heart
    and lean not on your own understanding;
in all your ways submit to him,
    and he will make your paths straight. Proverbs 3:5-6

I trust in you, Lord;
    I say, "You are my God."
My times are in your hands;
    deliver me from my enemies
    from those who pursue me. Psalm 31:14-15

Blessed is the one who trusts in the Lord Psalm 40:4a

In God I trust and am not afraid.
    What can man do to me? Psalm 56:11

You will keep in perfect peace
    those whose minds are steadfast,
    because they trust in you. Isaiah 26:3

Therefore I tell you, do not worry about your life, what you will eat or drink; or about your body, what you will wear. Is not life more than food, and the body more than clothes? Look at the birds of the air; they do not sow or reap or store away in barns, and yet your heavenly

Supplication

Father feeds them. Are you not much more valuable than they? Can any one of you by worrying add a single hour to your life?

And why do you worry about clothes? See how the flowers of the field grow. They do not labor or spin. Yet I tell you that not even Solomon in all his splendor was dressed like one of these. If that is how God clothes the grass of the field, which is here today and tomorrow is thrown into the fire, will he not much more clothe you—you of little faith? So do not worry, saying, 'What shall we eat?' or 'What shall we drink?' or 'What shall we wear?' For the pagans run after all these things, and your heavenly Father knows that you need them. But seek first his kingdom and his righteousness, and all these things will be given to you as well. Therefore do not worry about tomorrow, for tomorrow will worry about itself. Each day has enough trouble of its own. Matthew 6:25-33

Wisdom

In this information age it is easy to have a lot of knowledge, but still not know how to live. God's wisdom is very practical and often at odds with what unbelievers think is smart. Ask God to give you this wisdom and then pursue it by studying the Bible and putting it into practice.

> My goal is that [those who have not met Paul personally] may be encouraged in heart and united in love, so that they may have the full riches of complete understanding, in order that they may know the mystery of God, namely, Christ, in whom are hidden all the treasures of wisdom and knowledge. I tell you this so that no one may deceive you by fine-sounding arguments. Colossians 2:2-4

> Blessed are those who find wisdom,
>   those who gain understanding,
> for she is more profitable than silver
>   and yields better returns than gold.
> She is more precious than rubies;
>   nothing you desire can compare with her.
> Long life is in her right hand;
>   in her left hand are riches and honor.
> Her ways are pleasant ways,
>   and all her paths are peace.
> She is a tree of life to those who embrace her;
>   those who hold her fast will be blessed.
>   Proverbs 3:13-19

Whoever gives heed to instruction prospers,
    and blessed is he who trusts in the Lord. Proverbs 16:20

Hold on to instruction, do not let it go;
    guard it well, for it is your life. Proverbs 4:13

Those who trust in themselves are fools,
    but those who walk in wisdom are kept safe. Proverbs 28:26

Get wisdom, get understanding;
    do not forget my words or turn away from them.
Do not forsake wisdom, and she will protect you;
    love her, and she will watch over you.
The beginning of wisdom is this: Get wisdom.
    Though it cost all you have,
    get understanding. Proverbs 4:5-9

The fear of the Lord is the beginning of wisdom,
    all who follow his precepts
    have good understanding.
To him belongs eternal praise. Psalm 111:10

    If any of you lacks wisdom, you should ask God, who gives generously to all without finding fault, and it will be given to you. James 1:5

    Who is wise and understanding among you? Let them show it by their good life, by deeds done in the humility that comes from wisdom. But if you harbor bitter envy and selfish ambition in your hearts, do not boast about it or deny the truth. Such "wisdom" does not come down from heaven but is earthly, unspiritual, demonic. For where you have envy and selfish ambition, there you find disorder and every evil practice.

But the wisdom that comes from heaven is first of all pure; then peace-loving, considerate, submissive, full of mercy and good fruit, impartial and sincere. James 3:13-17

If you enjoyed this book, please consider leaving a
short review at Amazon.com
BarnesAndNoble.com
Goodreads.com
Bookbub.com
or another site of your choice.

Mentioning books on social media helps to
spread the word.
Your friends will thank you for the
recommendation.

Contact the author at leanne@leannehardy.net if you are interested in discounted prices of this book for bulk orders of ten or more for your church or small group.

An electronic version of this book is available for use on your phone or device.

For other books by LeAnne Hardy see
www.leannehardy.net

If you enjoyed this book, please consider leaving a short review at Amazon.com
BarnesAndNoble.com
Goodreads.com
Bookbub.com
or another site of your choice.

Mentioning books on social media helps to spread the word.
Your friends will thank you for the recommendation.

Contact the author at leanne@leannehardy.net if you are interested in discounted prices of this book for bulk orders of ten or more for your church or small group.

An electronic version of this book is available for use on your phone or device.

For other books by LeAnne Hardy see
www.leannehardy.net